NICKLAUS, PALMER, PLAYER, TREVINO

THE STORY OF ONE GREAT SEASON

TOUR '72

Michael D'Antonio

NEW YORK

ISBN: 0-7868-6716-7

Hyperion books are available for special promotions and
premiums. For details, contact Hyperion Special Markets, 77 W.
66th Street, 11th floor, New York, New York 10023-6298, or call
212-456-0100.

Book design by Caroline Cunningham

FIRST EDITION

10 9 8 7 6 5 4 3 2 1

For my father,

whose Hogan wedge—circa 1960—still gets me out of trouble

PRELUDE

Sports do not build character.
They reveal it.
−Heywood Hale Broun

Every champion inevitably meets his equal, and Arnold Daniel Palmer understood this truth. But in 1962, at the U.S. Open Championship, he was not ready to admit that Jack Nicklaus was the man, or that this was the moment. After all, they were playing at Oakmont Country Club near Pittsburgh, on Palmer's home turf. And Nicklaus had yet to show he had the stomach for an eighteen-hole, man-to-man play-off against the greatest player in the game.

No one attacked a golf course or an opponent like Palmer. He tried to drive every green, vault every tree, carry every lake. If you made birdie, he would answer with eagle. And if his bald aggression sent him into the rough, or the woods, he truly expected to follow with a dramatic recovery shot. The number of times he succeeded was astonishing. Whenever he hitched his trousers, flicked his cigarette to the ground, and imposed his will upon a golf ball, you expected a spectacular result.

Though his play was truly exceptional, Palmer would not have become a celebrity who transcended his sport if he wasn't also handsome and charismatic. While other golfers looked like your out-of-condition neighbor, Palmer had a half-back's physique and a movie idol's face. His eyes were bright blue, his jaw was square, and his dark hair was swept back. He was a hard drinker, a fast driver, and a daredevil pilot. Even the way he moved communicated his passion for life. Men and women alike flocked to be near that energy.

It would have been hard to imagine a topflight player more different from Palmer than Jack Nicklaus. Where Palmer was sleek, swift, and steely, Nicklaus was pudgy, plodding, and methodical. He was a stolid-looking youngster—thick legs, soft features, strangely small hands, short blond hair—with a squeaky voice that made him seem even younger than his years.

Those who underestimated Nicklaus didn't know the confidence he had gained as a very young player. By age nineteen, "I thought I must be a pretty good player because I had won the National Amateur and I was ranked as the number one amateur in the country," he recalled in 2001. "So I thought, 'I must be pretty decent.'"

In fact, young Nicklaus could smash the ball farther than almost anyone, and he was a superb, all-around player. And though he was sometimes criticized as a coddled country clubber, he was not rattled by the sort of class warfare waged against him, particularly by Palmer's most rabid fans. As much as they sought to typecast him as spoiled, or overly privileged,

Nicklaus believed to his core that he had earned his way to the top.

"None of those things would influence whether I really wanted to be a champion or not," said Nicklaus, referring to his early advantages. "I think that being a champion is the result of hard work. Did I resent it?" he asked, referring to the stereotype forced on him. "I didn't think it was probably a fair assumption of what my life truly was."

Fair or not, Arnie's "Army" cheered Nicklaus's mistakes and even stood in the woods holding signs that read, HIT IT HERE JACK. Palmer, who was nicknamed the King, was not above playing to the prejudices of the galleries. He referred to Nicklaus as "the fat boy." And a month before the Open, he noted that Nicklaus had failed to win a single tournament in his first five months as a pro. He went on to goad his young rival. "I'm beginning to wonder if he'll ever make it big as a pro," said Arnie. "He's got a tremendous weight problem, and he just doesn't seem to be working on his game as much as he should. To be a great player, you not only have to play tournaments, you have to practice all the time. That's the only way." Gary Player, also a star golfer, added, "Jack's a fine golfer, but he's still no Arnold Palmer."

Sometimes it seems like every man who had been alive in 1951 claims to have witnessed Bobby Thompson's home run, the shot-heard-round-the-world that sent the Giants to the World Series. So it is with golf fans and the 1962 U.S. Open. Everyone says they saw it. One man who actually did witness this bit of history, through eyes that understood it better than most, was Tom Weiskopf. Pressing up against the ropes that separated the huge gallery of 25,000 people from the players, twenty-year-old Weiskopf watched both men walk onto the first tee. He had expected confidence from Palmer, and he saw it. The surprise was Nicklaus. He seemed thoroughly at ease, as if he already knew what was going to happen.

Palmer teed up his ball and swung with every ounce of muscle he could employ. His drive screamed down the left side of the fairway. The cheering that followed was so long and loud that Weiskopf felt it in his stomach.

A few muffled boos greeted Nicklaus when his name was called on the first tee. He methodically palmed his ball and used it to press a white wooden tee into the turf. When he stood behind the teed-up ball, gathering his thoughts, visualizing the shot he would create, a look of focused determination came over his face. Though fans may not have noticed, the fat boy had shed twenty-five pounds in the previous six months. He was stronger and more flexible than ever.

Nicklaus stepped up to the ball. He waggled the club, and then coiled into a backswing that brought his left shoulder well past his chin. He seemed to pause for a split second before he unleashed, in perfect synchrony, all the power stored in his legs, torso, shoulders, and arms. The persimmon head of the club struck the ball with a loud crack that echoed sharply off the clubhouse, which was set one hundred yards behind the tee.

"Jack's ball just disappeared into the sky," recalled Weiskopf, who would himself become a PGA Tour champion. "I ran down the fairway to get ahead of them. Arnold took off fast, as always, but as he approached his own ball he continued to look down the fairway. He looked and looked, and his neck seemed to get longer, like an ostrich. Then his step slowed. He saw Jack's ball, a full twenty-five yards ahead of his. I could see it in Arnold's face. Jack had arrived."

Displaying a remarkable calm, Nicklaus proceeded from there to carefully carve up the course. He played every shot in the same calculated way. As he arrived at his ball he would pull a set of notes out of his back pocket and check his position against the distances he had measured from certain landmarks. (Nicklaus was among the first to record and use yardage notes. Over time, all the pros would come to rely on them.) After scanning his numbers, Nicklaus would select a club and stand, for a moment, until he could see the shot he wanted in his mind's eye. He would take a few practice swings, line himself up, and then adjust his body with waggles and shuffles. Refusing to swing until he felt just right, Nicklaus would sometimes take so long to play a stroke that he risked incurring a penalty for slow play.

He could be irritatingly slow, but the results were undeniable. In six quick holes Nicklaus gained four strokes. Over the full eighteen, Nicklaus hit every green but two in regulation. Palmer would attempt one of his famous charges on the back nine, but he would not be able to make up the deficit. Ironically, Nicklaus dominated the match with his putting, not his power. He only three-putted one green in the entire tournament. Palmer, the greatest clutch putter of the time, struggled on almost every green. Down two strokes on the eighteenth hole of the play-off, he desperately tried to hit the flagstick with his second shot. In the end he took a bogey six and then picked up his opponent's ball marker, signaling concession. Officials required Nicklaus to putt-out. As he retrieved his ball from the cup, the Oakmont gallery offered cheers and applause that were restrained, perhaps even grudging, given Nicklaus's superb performance.

After he had time in the locker room to digest his defeat, Palmer was asked about the outcome of his showdown with Nicklaus. He glanced at Nicklaus, who was a few feet away. "That big strong dude. I thought I was through with him yesterday." Palmer would never again call Nicklaus fat boy.

Arnold Palmer was not diminished by the rise of Jack Nicklaus. Instead, with a worthy opponent, his accomplishments became more significant. Though he lost that particular U.S. Open, 1962 would be one of Palmer's most successful years. It came to include wins at the Masters and the British Open. And in the ten years from 1962 to 1971 he would win thirty-four tournaments, including two more Majors. He would never lose the allegiance of his generation, those who became adults as the United States ended World War II and then grew into the richest and most powerful country the world had ever seen. Palmer was, for them, one of the faces of a bright and uncomplicated good time.

Only Nicklaus, with thirty-five U.S. victories and two British Opens, would best Palmer in the decade that followed their confrontation at Oakmont. Serious students of the game would see Nicklaus as the more complete player, the true heir to Bobby Jones, the great amateur who won the Grand Slam (four Majors in one year) in 1930 with a swing as close to perfect as had ever been seen. Nicklaus was as superior in his time as Jones had been in the 1920s and '30s. And no one ever dominated the Majors the way he did. Nicklaus would win eighteen

Major titles in his lifetime, establishing himself as the best individual athlete of the century, according to *Sports Illustrated*. Eventually he even earned his own nickname—the Golden Bear.

Together Nicklaus and Palmer made professional golf more exciting and popular than it had ever been. At the start of each year, sportswriters focused on the rivalry, and whenever both men appeared at a tournament, attendance and TV ratings rose. In the mid-1960s ten million people watched a typical tournament broadcast. More than twelve million, a record number, called themselves golfers.

Two big stars would have been enough to make this period in golf as memorable as any, but fans were often treated to unexpected thrills when the third dominant competitor of the time—Gary Player—entered a tournament. This happened at roughly a dozen events per year. A South African, Player was a credible challenge to the Nicklaus/Palmer axis. He was most dangerous at the Majors. At the 1961 Masters he scrambled to beat a charging Palmer for the second of what would one day be nine Major titles. In that same year he finished first on the American tour's money list, despite playing fewer than half the tournaments scheduled.

Just five feet seven inches tall, and weighing less than 150 pounds, dark-haired, square-jawed Player was the epitome of a scrappy competitor. While Nicklaus took Bobby Jones—elegant, graceful, elite—as a model, Player revered Ben Hogan, whose work ethic was truly self-punishing. If Player pushed himself as hard as he claimed, then he surely exceeded Hogan in his fanatical commitment to excel. When he left South Africa each winter, he packed sixty pounds of exercise weights in his luggage. (The weights and various other devices were part of his hotel room workouts.) He ran, practiced yoga, and held to a strict diet. While Nicklaus and Palmer both smoked and drank plenty, Player refused both of these indulgences. Even his trademark black clothes were calculated, at least in the beginning, to impart some competitive advantage. He believed they collected solar energy that his body could use.

Unlike other athletes of his time, Player willingly commented on issues outside sport. Journalists who generally tiptoed around the disgraceful treatment of black athletes by American golf, never demanding that Palmer or Nicklaus answer for it, went straight at Player on the issue of apartheid in his homeland. He became a target of protest and even death threats. While his peers worried about their putting strokes and rankings on the money list, Player spent too much of his time in the latter part of the decade arranging for bodyguards and checking to see if he was being followed.

Nothing would deter Player from his ambition. Doug Sanders, who joined the tour with Player in 1957, recalled an exchange they had that year over dinner at a coffee shop in Baton Rouge. Sanders asked Player if he gave him $250,000, which was an astronomical amount at that time, would he retire to a ranch in South Africa.

"I couldn't do that, laddie," replied Player.

"Why the hell not?" asked Sanders.

"Because I'm going to win all four Majors."

Three years after Jack Nicklaus publicly asserted his claim to being the greatest, Gary Player did much the same thing at Bellcrive Country Club, west of St. Louis. At the start of the 1965 U.S. Open, Player already held victories in the British Open (1959), the Masters (1961), and the PGA Championship (1962). The U.S. Open was the only premier event he hadn't won. If he could prevail at Bellerive, he would become just the third man in history, behind Hogan and Gene Sarazen, to claim all four Majors before reaching the age of thirty.

On the first day of play, on the first tee, Player glanced at the scoreboard and noted the names of previous champions, which had been posted by year. The space next to the year 1965 was blank, but Player saw his name written there, in gold letters. No one would have picked Player to win. The course was the longest in Open history, and the long hitters such as Nicklaus and Palmer were favored. But beginning with the moment he saw his name on the scoreboard, Player competed in a trancelike state of supreme grace and confidence. He won in a play-off with Kel Nagle, the Australian who had staved off Arnold Palmer to win the 1960 British Open.

The fourth Major established Player as roughly equal to Palmer and Nicklaus, and the trio was dubbed the Big Three. This term would become a marketing tool for their joint appearances and exhibition matches for years to come. Their domination of golf was incontestable. Between 1960 and 1967, Nicklaus, Palmer, and Player won every Masters but one, and a full fifteen of the twenty-eight Majors played.

While events in South Africa helped make Gary Player into a symbol of something old and sinister (in the eyes of some), they conspired to force a completely different role on the final great competitor to come of age in the late 1960s. A Mexican American, Lee Trevino was greeted by many minority fans as a standard-bearer, someone who would claim an exclusive corner of American life for them. At a time when people were cultivating ethnic pride and fighting for equal rights, many prominent members of minority groups were pressured to make themselves into symbols or role models. Many Hispanics wanted to turn the first golf star to spring from the ranks of poor Mexican Americans into an ethnic hero.

But Trevino was essentially apolitical, and no matter how many people hoped he might be a leader outside his sport, he never went much further than offhand remarks about crashing what was essentially an all-white party. If he said anything at all about being Mexican American, it was something self-effacing and nonthreatening. "Black may be beautiful, but brown is cute," he would say.

Though Trevino refused to be a spokesman for anything outside himself, what he said with his game was clear. The message was delivered first at yet another U.S. Open, the 1968 event, which was played at Oak Hill Country Club in Rochester, New York. This time, defending champion Nicklaus would fall, just as Palmer had five years earlier.

Given his relative anonymity, the press and spectators at Oak Hill didn't pay any more attention to Trevino's first-round score of 69 than they paid to the 70s carded by mid-rank pros Dave Marr and Labron Harris, Jr. And though Trevino followed up with a 68 on day two, he was still overshadowed. Bert Yancey, a more widely respected player, had scored just as well, holding on to the lead. And Nicklaus, moving up the leaderboard, seemed poised to catch him.

The gallery's purists, looking for the most beautiful swing, no doubt followed Nicklaus or Yancey. But those who wanted sheer entertainment flocked to Trevino. By round three, every fan knew that he put on a show of both golf and personality. Almost every shot was preceded by a quip to his caddie or an aside to the people behind the ropes that held back the gallery. Typical was this: "I used to be a Mexican, but I'm makin' money now, so I'm gonna be a Spaniard."

Trevino's good shots were followed by huge grins and the occasional dance step. Mis-hits typically led to creative recoveries. A good example came on the seventeenth hole of the third round. Continuing the approach that had served him so far, Trevino had been aggressive from the start of the round and managed to gain a stroke, cutting Yancey's lead to one. But his tee shot on the par-four hole number seventeen flew wide of the fairway and landed in rough that, typical of the U.S. Open, was long and gnarly. Refusing the safe play—a wedge back onto the short grass—he swung a long iron for the green. The ball ended up to the right of the putting surface, just above a greenside bunker.

Up there beside the green, Trevino's ball was tangled in rough again, and he had a severely sloping lie. The only way he could get to the ball was to plant his left foot in the sand and his right foot well above it in the grass. Somehow he managed to firmly and yet smoothly swing the clubhead through the grass and under the ball. It popped up, fell with a hollow thud, and then rolled straight at the cup, which was a good forty feet away. It didn't stop rolling until it was within a foot of the hole.

Watching this from beside the green, Yancey appeared shocked and then disbelieving. Trevino had been in trouble, facing a certain bogey, maybe even a double. Yancey had put his own second shot within twelve feet and seemed destined to pick up another stroke, or two, on his pursuer. Now, Trevino's par was guaranteed. Yancey lined up to the ball, made a couple of practice strokes, and missed. After both men parred the final hole, they faced a Sunday championship round with Yancey leading by the slenderest margin. For his part, Trevino had an opportunity to become the first player in U.S. Open history to card four rounds under 70.

On the last day of the 1968 U.S. Open, the most important round of golf in his life, Lee Trevino showed up wearing a screaming red shirt with matching socks that flashed from under a pair of black trousers with cuffs cut so high that they would have fit someone two inches shorter. For an extra dash of spice, he pulled a bright red leather golf glove onto his left hand.

The gallery had fallen for him, and when he arrived he heard shouts of encouragement, even cries of "beat the gringo." He signed autographs and joked with the officials.

Bert Yancey appeared on the first tee with huge crescents of sweat staining his pale blue shirt. His face was as white as the visor on his head. While Trevino chatted with the gallery, Yancey stared at the ground. When it came time to play, he hit a careful, precise drive. Trevino whacked at the ball so hard that he almost fell over on his follow-through.

Trevino's instinct told him that Yancey was likely to beat himself, and that he should watch out for Jack Nicklaus. He was right. By the tenth hole Trevino was four shots up on Yancey and began to think about breaking records. All he had to do was score pars on the final four holes and he would become the first player to break par in all four rounds of the U.S. Open. He would also tie Nicklaus for the lowest total score—275—ever recorded at the Open tournament.

The first two pars came easily, then the tension took hold. On the sixteenth tee Trevino hit a crooked drive into the rough on the left side, but a strong seven iron to the center of the green saved him. On number seventeen he hit a big drive but sculled his two iron, catching only the top half of the ball with his club and sending it skittering forward. He then hit a poor chip, and needed to make a fifteen-footer for par. He made it and went to the final hole with a chance at both records.

As they stood on the tee of the par four, the young caddie who had seen Trevino through the tournament told him to swing as hard as he could. Trevino pulled up his red socks, spit on his hands, and then swung so hard that, again, his follow-through almost pulled him over. The shot was long, but also left, and it landed in thick rough. When they got to it, they could see that the ball was settled deep into the grass. The caddie had more to say.

"You don't want to be remembered," he whispered, "as the 1968 U.S. Open champion who laid up on the eighteenth hole."

A less emotional player might have played safe, hacking the ball back onto the fairway and then taking a clear shot at the green. Trevino grabbed a six iron and went for the pin. U.S. Open courses are known for rough that is so long and thick it can slow anyone's swing, and when Trevino's iron came down, the grass grabbed it and almost stopped it. When the club face finally made contact, the ball just popped up, flew a few yards, and then settled back into the thick stuff.

Undaunted, Trevino took a wide stance beside the ball, a sand wedge in his hand. He made another, lashing swing and then stood back as the ball flew higher and farther than he could have hoped. It finally came to rest on the right side of the green, just four feet from the hole, four feet from two U.S. Open records. He walked the last one hundred yards of the fairway with the applause and cheers of 5,000 fans echoing in his ears.

As he stood over the putt, Lee Trevino, driving range impresario, thought it was the longest four-footer he'd ever seen. He could see dangerous breaks, bumps, and spikemarks, which could all push the ball off its path to the hole. No one watching Trevino knew this short putt looked to him like a twenty-five-foot challenge with ten feet of break. And nothing in his stroke betrayed his fear. He squared himself and without hesitation smoothly rolled the ball into the hole. He was the champion.

Though some considered him a loudmouthed, one-win wonder, Trevino's game and his patter would hold up over the long run. Trevino talked before, after, and sometimes in the middle of his own swing. "We don't have to talk," he would tell other players who expressed their annoyance. "You just have to listen." At a World Cup match, he settled over a putt and while the gallery grew quiet, he just kept talking. "With a million-dollar swing like mine," he said, drawing the blade back, "I can't miss." He hit the ball on the word "miss" and it rolled right in. Fans loved it.

The 1968 U.S. Open brought Lee Trevino to the top of the world of golf, alongside Nicklaus, Palmer, Player, and a few other extraordinary players such as Billy Casper and Tom Watson. When the final analyses of the twentieth-century game were written, some thirty-plus years later, this period would be regarded as a pinnacle. At no time would a greater number of the game's best compete on such equal footing. The rivalry was intense, and often personal. Palmer and Nicklaus maintained a public amity but were not close friends, and each burned to defeat the other. Trevino made no secret of his admiration for Nicklaus, but he also lived to beat him. "As long as I can beat him, I feel all right," he would say in the middle of 1972. "If he finishes thirteenth and I finish twelfth, I feel like I've defeated somebody besides myself."

Of course, sport does not live in isolation, and it's important to note that in the late 1960s and early 1970s, America endured tumultuous social change. In 1968, the assassinations of Martin Luther King, Jr., and Robert Kennedy stunned the nation. In that same year, the Tet offensive forced Americans to doubt their country's purpose in Vietnam. Feminism, the sexual revolution, the civil rights movement, and even psychedelic pop culture challenged the status quo.

"Drugs, crime, campus revolution, racial discord, draft resistance," complained President Richard Nixon. "On every hand we find old standards violated, old values discarded, old principles ignored."

The turmoil of the times did affect some athletes. The 1968 Olympics will be remembered forever as the games where African American medal winners raised their fists in Black Power salutes. But while some joined in the social conflict, most athletes lived in splendid isolation from the turmoil of their times, and their performances provided an escape for spectators. The sports page relieved everyone from the troubles on the front page. In sport, the traditional rules of play still held.

This was especially true in the game of golf. Sure, players grew their hair. Their sideburns sprouted. But the game was played by the same ancient rules, on the same courses, in the same conditions. It was stable. And perhaps for this reason, it attracted more and more people. In this period, millions of Americans took up the game. Record numbers of tournaments were broadcast on TV. And golfers became some of the best-paid athletes in all of sport. With their winnings, endorsements, real estate, and golf course design businesses, Palmer, Nicklaus, Player, and Trevino all made more per year than the highest-salaried baseball or football players.

Together these men created a Golden Age of Golf. It would culminate in the 1972 season, a moment in the game's history when competition reached its very highest level. No other year could claim so many of the sport's all-time greats. No other season would contain so many dramatic moments, exhilarating highs, and shocking surprises. By the time it was over, the '72 tour would, for generations, define many of golf's legendary personalities and display the game at its best.

CHAPTER 1

I think Nicklaus is capable of it. But I think there
are players capable of stopping him.
—PGA commissioner Joe Dey, on the Slam
March 1972

As 1972 began, Lee Trevino's perfect smile beamed out at America from the cover of *Sports Illustrated*. It was a familiar pose, all white teeth and mischievous brown eyes, and it hid completely the fear and doubt lurking within golf's new hero. "No one knew but me that I was worried stiff that it had all been a fluke," Trevino would confess thirty years later. "I went into the year trying to answer one question for myself. 'Am I really that good?' "

As the *SI* cover announced, Trevino had been named the magazine's Sportsman of the Year, one of the highest honors an American athlete could receive. He won despite the fact that the year had also seen the Ali–Frazier "Fight of the Century"— Frazier won in fifteen rounds—and Kareem Abdul-Jabbar's rise to dominance in pro basketball. The award acknowledged that Trevino had crafted what was perhaps the best one-month run of golf in history, winning the U.S., Canadian, and British Opens.

The magnificent trifecta began at the ancient Merion Golf Club on Philadelphia's Main Line. Though short by modern standards, Merion posed an intimidating array of obstacles, including narrow fairways, thick woods, slick greens, and more than 125 bunkers. After the tournament Trevino would admit he approached the course "with a twinge of fear" because he knew "every shot had to be played well."

For most of the tournament, the gallery had been focused on Jim Simons, a tall blond college student who had bolted into the lead in the first round and held it until Sunday. After three rounds it seemed that Simons would become the first amateur to win the U.S. Open since Johnny Goodman in 1933. But then rain arrived to soften the greens, making them receptive to Trevino's low shots, which he fired close to the flagsticks. After the final round of the weekend, Simons was gone and it was Trevino and Nicklaus tied for the lead and bound, by fate, to settle the championship in a play-off.

Many people would remember the play-off at Merion for the rubber snake that Trevino pulled out of his golf bag on the first tee and flipped at Nicklaus. For the record, Nicklaus wasn't bothered by the gag, and even some of the buttoned-down USGA officials laughed. But the incident did set a playful tone for the 10,000 spectators, who seemed to immediately join Trevino's side. And maybe the gallery gave him a psychological edge.

Anyone who had seen Trevino at the 1968 Open, and

then at this one, would have noticed that he had become a far more comfortable and polished player. He didn't spend much time listening to his caddie or suffering over putts. His step was confident. His swing was steady. His clothes—this time he wore a spotless white shirt, black pants, and matching saddle shoes—fit perfectly.

Time and again he saved himself from the rough and from greenside bunkers to make clutch pars and birdies. In contrast, Nicklaus seemed tentative, especially when he dug into the soft white silica in Merion's bunkers. He surprised the gallery when he flubbed a sand shot on hole number two and failed even to get out of the bunker. He downright shocked them when he did it a second time on the very next hole. (Trevino would later cite these events as proof that "the good Lord doesn't give you everything." In this case, He hadn't blessed Nicklaus with a solid sand game.)

On the third hole, a par three, both players drove into a bunker on the left side of the green. Trevino waltzed in, quickly punched at his ball, and landed it within six feet of the hole. Nicklaus then shuffled around in the sand, settled uncomfortably, and hit a weak low shot that never cleared the far edge of the hazard. When this happened, his reaction was not so different from what you'd see from a weekend hacker. First, his whole body slumped. Then, for a long moment he didn't move at all. He just stared down into the sand as if he might discover that the swing had been a fantasy and the ball was really still there, at his feet, waiting to be struck.

From that moment on, the result of the match seemed almost predestined. Nicklaus became more tentative. He nearly drove the green on hole number ten, a 312-yard par four. But then he chunked his pitch, hitting the turf before the ball. It didn't even reach the green. Instead of a sure birdie, he made bogey. Trevino made a twenty-five-footer on hole number twelve, and an even longer putt on fifteen to go three shots up. As Trevino grew increasingly confident, the strain showed on Nicklaus's face. It was the faraway look of fear, the same look that Tom Weiskopf had seen in Arnold Palmer's eyes when Nicklaus outdrove him at Oakmont in 1962.

After the match, Trevino was careful to reduce the expectations he might put on himself and keep fans focused on his opponent. He was already thinking about the next time they would meet. "I'm a lucky dog," he yelped. "You gotta be lucky to beat Jack Nicklaus, because he's the greatest golfer to ever hold a club."

With the U.S. Open trophy captured, Trevino went to Quebec and seized the Canadian Open in a sudden-death play-off with Art Wall. He won with an eighteen-foot putt on the very first hole. In accounts of the tournament, sportswriters made special note of the fans who fled Arnie's Army when "Señor Lee Trevino" was announced on the first tee.

(Ten years earlier, the very idea that anyone would desert Palmer would have been hard to accept. But by 1972, even he could not deny that age and the demands of simply being Arnold Palmer were having their effects. As he had amassed sixty tournament victories worldwide, including seven Majors, Palmer had also acquired a huge and demanding business empire and a bad hip joint. His practice time, physical energy, and intellectual focus were all taxed. Palmer's last Major win had come at the 1964 Masters.)

After Canada, Trevino traveled to Royal Birkdale Golf Club in Lancashire where British Open fans actually booed him during his third round matchup with their nation's standard-bearer, Tony Jacklin. Unfazed, Trevino won the tournament, beating Jacklin by two and Lu Liang Huan of Taiwan by a single stroke.

With his third Major title in three years, Trevino was the hottest golfer alive. All over the country, blue-collar fans swelled with pride over Trevino's dominance of the gilded game. Halfway between Dallas and Austin, in the little city of Temple, a supermarket clerk named Paul Guillen celebrated the success of *El Super-Mexicano* with friends at the clubhouse of the local public course.

"He was for *us*, for the guys who played on sand greens and paid six bucks a round," recalled Guillen, years later. "We were all Lee's Fleas, I guess. Arnold had the Army. Lee had the Fleas. He made us feel like it could be done. Like one of us could make it."

Being the first brown-skinned superstar in golf set Trevino up for certain pressures that white athletes rarely faced. Other minority sports figures, most notably Muhammad Ali, used their fame to advance their views on race and politics. Ali had stood against the Vietnam War and in favor of black political aspirations. In the late 1960s and early 1970s it was common for young African American athletes to promote social issues.

But though black America was deeply and fully engaged in racial politics, the same was not true for Mexican Americans. Immigration problems and language barriers had likely led to a certain reluctance to challenge white authorities. Whatever the cause, like most Mexican Americans, Trevino was reluctant to join ethnic leaders who were trying to spur civil rights activism in Hispanic communities. When asked to aid a special project for Mexican Americans in his home state of Texas he would answer, "No blacks allowed in? No Jews?" If such was the case, he wanted no part.

If Trevino identified with any group, it was not Mexican Americans but rather *all* of the poor and lower middle class who struggled as he did. Trevino had been born into "the kind of family, that well, like, we were existing and that was all." He never knew his father and was never educated past the seventh grade. "I was probably dyslexic," he would say as an adult. "I sure know I had what they call attention deficit disorder. But they didn't know about those things then. So I just got stuck in the back of the class. I listened, and I watched, and I saw that the louder ones, the funny ones, got the most attention." He dropped out of school at age fourteen to work at a golf course, Glen Lakes, which was near the four-room house he was raised in.

In his teen years, Trevino had been a bully and a loud-mouth. But his antics stopped just short of the kind of criminal activity that got many of his peers in real trouble. "The worst thing was when this buddy of mine stole some hubcaps off of this powder blue '49 Ford that was in the parking lot at the golf course," recalls Trevino. "They were perfect for my car and we put them on. Well, the owner reports them missing to the police and the club pro. I'm driving around with them and the cops stop me right away. The officer says, 'Nice hubcaps. Where'd you get 'em?' Before I can answer he tells me that if they're returned immediately, things will be all right. I took them to the guy, gave them to him face-to-face, crying like a baby."

As it is today, the military then was both a haven and a step toward the middle class for many poor young men, and Trevino took it, lying about his age in order to enlist in the Marines. (Later he would say that the Marines kept him out of prison.) While Nicklaus was in college at Ohio State, Trevino was a grunt in Okinawa whose claim to fame was that he held the title as best machine gunner in the Third Division. After his discharge in 1960 he went home to North Dallas and took a job at a driving range and pitch-and-putt course called Hardy's. He built his own game there and survived by gambling in low-stakes matches with the toughest competitors around—the kind that need the money. He wasn't thinking about future U.S. Opens. He was thinking about food and rent. "My intentions were to beat those guys I played with at one o'clock every day. They'd be waiting for me to get off so we could tee it up, and we would go out there and play twenty-five-cent skins." In a single day, these small bets could add up to a month's rent.

When he made it big on the PGA Tour, Trevino saw the same men he beat for $5 bets in his galleries cheering and drinking beer. "I represent the guy who goes to the driving range, the municipal player, the truck driver, the union man, the guy who grinds it out. To them, I am someone who worked hard, kept at it, and made it. Sure I go out of my way to talk to them. They're my people."

Trevino's people had enjoyed three full years of their man's chatter and his dominance on the course. Through 1971 he had won nine times and twice captured the tour's annual Vardon Trophy for lowest average score on tour. He won more than $200,000, which was an impressive sum at a time when a complete set of golf clubs could be had for $79. This success in tournaments translated into lucrative endorsement deals and business projects. He signed with Dr Pepper, Chrysler, Stylist Shoe Company, and Downtowner Motor Inns. There was even an apartment complex—Casa Trevino—under construction in El Paso.

Success affected Trevino in some negative ways. The arguments with his wife, Claudia, grew more frequent and more intense, so much so that they were often rumored to be separated. And if he didn't actually drink more, people noticed it more. When he reportedly overslept his starting time and was disqualified from the 1970 Westchester Classic, it was because he had stayed too late at some New York nightspots. A year later, at the same tournament, he confessed to a friend, "I can't think anymore. I'm in a daze." Arnold Palmer, who won the $50,000 first prize after Trevino missed the cut, offered this observation: "He's just finding out what it's like. Nobody can play at that pace and stay on top. It takes its toll."

No matter the toll his achievements took on him personally, all of golf took pleasure in the fact that Trevino was recognized as Sportsman of the Year in a competition that included every kind of athlete, from football linemen to track-

and-field stars. Golfers have always been sensitive to the suspicion, held by many, that they are not really athletes on the same level as, say, ballplayers or boxers. To have a national magazine place *any* golfer at the top of the sports world was vindication for the game as a whole.

Sadly, as the game welcomed a new man of the moment, it lost a hero for the ages. In December 1971, the wife and children of Robert Tyre Jones gathered at his bedside to witness his dying. Fans and friends had long known that Jones, then sixty-nine years old, was in decline. Diagnosed in 1956 with a degenerative spinal cord disease, he had gone from cane to wheelchair, and finally, to bed. It had been five years since he had been well enough to go out on a golf course, even in a cart. Jones's suffering was recorded in letters to his doctors. In one he explained that his life was as "miserable as one could imagine." By the time he drew his last breath, on December 18, 1971, death was a relief.

For many in golf, death transformed Jones immediately from legend to saint. His accomplishments did cast a huge shadow over the game. Born and raised in Atlanta, at age fourteen Jones had reached the quarterfinals of the 1916 U.S. Amateur Championship. In 1923, he began a never-equaled string of four wins and eight seconds in eight U.S. Open Championships. In 1930, he won the U.S. Open, then went to Great Britain to win the Amateur and Open titles. Jones's victory at the U.S. Amateur, on the same treacherous Merion course where Trevino beat Nicklaus in 1971, completed the Grand Slam of all four Majors in a single year. He promptly retired from competitive golf. He was twenty-eight years old.

Long deemed impossible, the Grand Slam won by Jones was celebrated by a nation mired in the Great Depression. When he returned from Britain, Jones got a homecoming parade in New York and a huge contract to produce instructional films. Over time, the press and his other admirers turned Jones into an idol, placing him on a pedestal as high as the ones that held Ruth, Grange, and Tunney. The public's admiration was fed by Jones's steadfast commitment to remaining an amateur. Many believed his refusal to accept pay for his play lent an air of purity to his accomplishments. He did it all for love of the game, and nothing else, and this only increased the power of his legend.

In order to nurture the myth, much of what was real about Jones was ignored by many of his admirers. On the golf course he threw clubs and swore. (These habits faded as he aged.) Away from it, he drank and smoked to excess. He was barely tolerant of small children and babies, even his own. As the creator of the Masters and Augusta National Golf Club, long bastions of racial exclusion, Jones helped maintain the game's elitism and bigotry. He would police the behavior of the competitors at the Masters and sometimes sent post-tournament notes admonishing those who had transgressed his notions of decorum.

The unpleasant side of Jones was routinely ignored by the press. Reporters referred to him in all seriousness as "Emperor Jones" and devoted thousands of words to the construction of his myth. Paul Gallico of the New York *Daily News* shamelessly called Jones "my hero." As the years passed, the Jones legend was expanded, rebuilt, and added onto like an old Southern manse. The idea of Jones became so impossibly grand, and revered, that it became widely accepted that no one would ever match his feats or the quality of his character. Upon his death, one *New York Times* column was titled "Man Who Approached Perfection."

One of those who had always believed in Bobby Jones was Louis Charles Nicklaus. In 1926, Charlie Nicklaus was a twelve-year-old boy caught up in the excitement as the U.S. Open came to his hometown of Columbus, Ohio, and the Scioto Country Club. Earlier in the year, Jones had been trounced by Walter Hagen, the top professional of the time. Ever relaxed, and wholly devoted to the pursuit of pleasure, Hagen was the anti-Jones, and fans made a clear statement about their values as they identified with one or the other. Jones stood for purity and sheer goodness. Hagen represented flash and polish. He loved beautiful women, beautiful cars, and beautiful clothes. After he won the match, by a very large margin, he sent Jones a pair of beautiful gold cuff links.

After his loss to Hagen, Jones had practiced hard and won the British Open. He returned to the States determined to wipe out the public memory of Hagen's triumph by winning the Open at Scioto. An idealistic young Charlie Nicklaus adopted Jones as his hero and watched him play every shot of the seventy-two-hole tournament. The last round was played under low-hanging clouds that seemed ready to pour at any moment. As Hagen faded, Jones reached the final nine holes of play in second place, four shots behind professional Joe Turnesa. As Turnesa stumbled to a back-nine score of 40, Jones rallied with spectacular play that included a 300-yard drive on the finishing hole. In victory he became the first man to ever hold the British and U.S. Open titles simultaneously.

Following the match, as a crowd of 6,000 cheered Jones outside, Hagen complained sourly to his fellow pros in the locker room. "Whenever I fail to stop Jones," he chided, "the rest of you curl up and die."

While Hagen snorted and fumed, many in the gallery, Charlie Nicklaus included, were awestruck. Charlie would grow up, go to college, become a successful local druggist, tennis champ of Columbus, and semi-pro football player. But even in adulthood, he never stopped worshiping Bobby Jones. Twenty years after he tagged along with Jones at Scioto, when Charlie Nicklaus's own ten-year-old son decided he might like to play golf, there was no question in his father's mind about who might serve as a role model. It would be the great Bobby Jones.

In an interview in 2001, Jack Nicklaus said, "Bobby Jones was an idol to me, and a standard by which I measured my career." In fact, Jones, or rather the oversized myth of Jones, loomed over Jack Nicklaus from the moment he began playing at the Scioto Country Club in Columbus, Ohio. An oil portrait of Jones hung in the Scioto locker room, and the older members of the club never tired of describing how he had hit this shot or that putt during the 1926 Open. Charlie raised his son according to the idealized Jones's example in all things, both on the course and off. Whenever Jack seemed even a little bit self-impressed, Charlie would relieve the swelling in his head by recounting Jones's record. "That usually did the trick," Jack admitted as an adult.

Besides pushing his son to excel, Charlie Nicklaus was a prosperous businessman, providing Jack with a sheltered life in the comfortable Columbus suburb of Upper Arlington. Similar to Scarsdale in New York or Winnetka outside Chicago, Upper Arlington reflected the wealth and comfort of upper-middle-class America in the 1950s. The town had a neat little commercial center with shops in Tudor-style buildings. Its older houses were large, Victorian-era masterpieces. Its new subdivisions were no Levittowns but rather tasteful treed communities of sprawling one-story homes and mini-mansions. Schools in the town were first-rate, and the children were cherished. An example of this positive attitude can be found on little Jack Nicklaus's report card from third grade. "Jack's work and conduct are good," writes his teacher, "and that is not always true of boys as lively as he is."

The center of social life in Upper Arlington was Scioto Country Club. Everything at the club was top-notch. A sprawling brick clubhouse was perfect for dinner dances and wedding receptions. At its swimming pool, the children of Upper Arlington could learn to paddle under the eye of a former coach of the U.S. Olympic swim team. Scioto's golf course had some of the best facilities for practice anywhere, including a large grass range. It was there, between swims and sandwiches at the cabana, that Jack Nicklaus honed his skills.

The very first pro who gave Nicklaus a lesson, Scioto's Jack Grout, became his teacher for life. "Jack Grout was there for me from the day I picked up a club at age ten at Scioto until he passed away in 1989," Nicklaus would recall. Grout's weathered face, rimless glasses, and habit of wearing a coat and tie on the course could make him seem overly serious. But in fact he was an exceedingly kind and soft-spoken man whose philosophy connected the game and life itself. He said that both rewarded "patience, self-control, and honest self-analysis." And both punished "anger and self-deception."

Grout, who was forty years old when he first saw Nicklaus, emphasized the basic elements of the swing—grip, posture, alignment—even for his most gifted students. And Nicklaus was, from almost the start, the most gifted young player Grout would ever see. Because young Jack Nicklaus was highly co-ordinated but also powerful, Grout let him swing as hard as he wanted to, and then taught him how to control the ball's flight. He gave him an interlocking grip, to accommodate his small hands, and a solid stance that permitted the stoutly built boy to use all the strength in his legs and torso.

Through the early 1950s, Nicklaus and a group of boys took lessons together at Scioto from Grout. Invariably Grout would pause in the middle of his instructions and say, "Jackie, show them how it's done." Jack would then fire off a shot with the kind of precision and power that none of the other boys could ever hope to develop. Nicklaus paid a price for these displays later, in the club's swimming pool, where the other boys made sure to push him underwater as often as they could. For his part, Grout offered Nicklaus a fatherly kind of love, and motivation. Whenever he saw Nicklaus practicing he was likely to say, "Let's go Jackie Buck, you're fifteen thousand balls behind."

By age thirteen, Nicklaus had shot 69 three times on the

demanding Scioto course. (The best Jones had done when he won the Open there was 70.) As his talent became apparent, sportswriters began, as early as 1950, to compare Nicklaus to his role model. No one since Jones had shown so much ability at such a young age. The two met for the first time at the United States Golf Association's National Amateur Championship of 1955 in Virginia, when Nicklaus was just fifteen. Jones appeared in a golf cart on the eleventh hole, just as the youngster was stepping up to his tee shot. Nicklaus responded with two bogeys, and then a double bogey to lose his match by one.

Of course, a single nervous outing in front of Bobby Jones did not prevent Nicklaus from winning all manner of amateur championships against boys and men. Before he left college, Nicklaus won two national amateur championships. In 1960, two years before he would turn professional, Nicklaus the amateur was already good enough to lead the U.S. Open on the final day and finish second by just two strokes. When he finally arrived on the pro tour in 1962, he was regarded as the only man alive with a real chance to replicate the Slam.

So it was that all along, Jack Nicklaus had competed against both the flesh-and-blood golfers in every tournament field and the impossibly perfect myth of Jones. His own goal was to match or even succeed Jones in the Majors and in the eyes of history. The pursuit had to be exhausting. And by the late 1960s, the strain showed. In 1968 and 1969 he won just four times. By his own account he had grown a little lazy, a little complacent. Many sportswriters began to ask, in print, "What's wrong with Jack?"

What was wrong probably had more to do with Nicklaus

the private man than with the athlete who performed for the gallery. In December 1969, Nicklaus had been shaken by the news that his father—his cheerleader, adviser, and friend—had been diagnosed with incurable pancreatic cancer. Never before exposed to serious illness, he was distressed by his father's rapid decline and found it almost unbearable to stand witness. When unable to visit himself, he pressed friends and family to monitor Charlie's condition and keep him informed. Cancer killed Charlie Nicklaus on February 19, 1970. He was just fifty-six years old.

With his father's passing, and then the death in December 1971 of Bobby Jones, Nicklaus was, for the first time, without his heroes. He regretted that he had recently let his practice routine slip. For a couple of years he had depended on his innate talent instead of hard work. And while he had played well, he had not dominated the tour in the same way as he had before.

"My dad had lived to watch me play golf," he would say, "and I felt I had let him down." But in the absence of his guiding lights, Nicklaus was also, at last, growing into a mature man. Being almost twenty years older than Nicklaus, Larry O'Brien was able to see this happening. A veteran sports journalist, O'Brien had been hired by Nicklaus to handle the hordes of reporters who covered his every move, and he quickly became one of the golfer's closest associates. It was O'Brien who had called with the news of Jones's death.

"It affected him greatly," O'Brien would eventually recall. "But I think that losing his father and Jones also pushed him into being more of an adult. He was thirty-two years old. He had a family of his own and, for the first time, no one but himself to rely on. It changed him."

The change was most visible away from the golf course, when Nicklaus allowed himself to reflect on his life. Virtually alone among his peers, he would question whether athletes should receive such large sums of money for playing games. He actually thought about whether he was worthy of the acclaim he received and allowed himself to ask, aloud, "Am I that good?" No one else in golf was secure enough to say these kinds of things out loud.

Nicklaus was also willing to examine his attitude and admit he didn't like what he saw. For three years he had been trying to get by mainly on his natural talent, often neglecting practice and preparation. Others, notably Trevino, had risen to challenge his dominance of the PGA Tour. In one particularly bad eight-week stretch, Nicklaus had played like a journeyman, getting himself cut from two of the five events he played, and earning a grand total of $5,259.17 in the three he completed. "I hadn't worked as hard as I should have," he later confessed. "I'd wasted time. I had to get my rear end in gear and get ready to go play."

As part of his renewal, Nicklaus decided to shed, once and for all, the extra pounds that had bothered him since college. If he didn't quite fit the medical definition, Nicklaus considered himself a compulsive eater. He ate all the time and found great comfort in food. (On the very first page of his 1997 autobiography, Nicklaus makes mention of a hot fudge sundae.) If he was going to stop eating so much, he would need help. Weight loss was not yet the national obsession it came to be. Little information on dieting was available. The best-known program at the time was Weight Watchers—a friend had lost thirty pounds on it—so that was where Nicklaus turned.

But there was a problem. The famous Jack Nicklaus couldn't comfortably stroll into one of the weekly meetings that were the heart of the Weight Watchers behavior modification strategy. So he asked his wife, Barbara, to copy the Weight Watchers menu for his meals, and he applied the same power of will he used on the golf course to his appetite. As a further spur, he invited the tailors from a clothing manufacturer that was his sponsor to visit in two and a half weeks to measure him for a new wardrobe. The diet and willpower worked, steadily stripping off the layers of fat he had carried for years. He got his new wardrobe, and Barbara Nicklaus got a husband she would describe as perhaps a little "too cute" for her comfort.

As Nicklaus worked on his physical image, he also poured effort into his game. No one was a more devoted student of the golf swing, and few players were more capable of self-criticism. In the off-season, he was determined to examine every delicate piece of his swing. Like a soldier preparing his carbine on the night before battle, he would disassemble it, inspect it, and carefully restore it to its most perfect condition.

Jack Grout, who by 1971 had moved to a course not far from Nicklaus's home in North Palm Beach, Florida, helped with the off-season tune-up. "Dr. Grout," as he was often called by the Nicklaus crowd, seemed able to repair any flaw in his prize student's swing. He could even diagnose Nicklaus's problems over the phone and prescribe fixes. Some of those who were close to the two men believed that sometimes the sound of Grout's voice—more than the content of his comments—was the important part of the cure.

Long after his PGA Tour days were over, Nicklaus acknowledged that Jack Grout became even more important in the early 1970s. "Like my dad he was both a friend and a mentor," recalled Nicklaus. "And after my father's death, Jack truly became like a second father to me."

Between the 1971 and '72 seasons, Grout spent long hours with his favorite pupil, shoring up both his heart and his game. On the practice tee he checked everything from grip and stance to the way Nicklaus shifted his weight. He always taught that on the backswing, a right-handed player's weight should roll into his right heel. On the downswing it should be moved to the inside of the left ankle. This move stored and then unleashed the power that Nicklaus used to intimidate other players and overwhelm certain golf courses, such as Augusta National.

Grout was also essential to building Nicklaus's confidence. As difficult as it would have been for his competitors to believe, Nicklaus was subject to ordinary self-doubt and worry. Those close to him saw it, and in the off-season before the 1972 PGA Tour they knew that Nicklaus's main worry had a name: Trevino. "Jack was absolutely terrified of him," recalls golf course architect Desmond Muirhead, a Nicklaus friend at the time.

"Trevino was probably the superior athlete. He was more creative, and he could go on a tear that would put him at the top for weeks. Up until 1972, Jack had never won two tournaments in a row. He didn't have the ability to go on a hot streak the way that Trevino did. Trevino scared him to death."

If Trevino's challenge wasn't enough, Nicklaus began the year by making a bold declaration that added enormously to the average sports fan's interest in the coming season. In a joint interview with Trevino, he actually announced to the magazine *Golf Digest* that the Slam was his goal for 1972. He explained that the Majors would all be held at courses he loved and played well—the Masters at Augusta, the U.S. Open at Pebble Beach, the British at Muirfield, and the PGA at Oakland Hills. He might never have a better opportunity to match Emperor Bobby.

Nicklaus had already planned his entire year—when he would play in tournaments, his practice schedule, his vacations—in order to peak for each of the Majors. Ever mindful that he was competing with Jones, Nicklaus knew he would forever be judged by the number of Major titles he won. Fourteen years into his quest, he was still two victories behind the record thirteen that Jones had won in eight years.

Thirty years later, Trevino would look back at 1972 and say that Nicklaus had to go for the Slam because he needed the challenge. "He was so good that regular challenges didn't motivate him," he said. "He had to set a goal like that to get his juices flowing." At the time, however, about all Trevino could say about the Nicklaus quest was, "I don't think it's possible for me, but it may be for Jack." Once again, the stage was set for Trevino to play the lovable everyman while Jack Nicklaus pursued a place in history. For himself, Trevino quietly set a more ordinary, but nevertheless ambitious goal. He wanted to be number one on the tour's money list come the end of 1972.

The 1972 tour began, officially, with the Glen Campbell–Los Angeles Open at little Rancho Park municipal golf course, across from a movie studio in West Hollywood. The favorites were Palmer and Trevino. Like Player and Nicklaus, they attracted attention wherever they teed up a ball. But in Palmer's case, at least, the galleries were on notice that they should expect something new from the old Palmer.

In January, Palmer had reflected on the slow decline of his winnings and on his even more discouraging record in the Majors. The Majors were the real prizes in the world of golf, and Palmer had to recognize that there were times when his style cost him in these events. The best example was probably the 1966 U.S. Open at the Olympic Club in San Francisco, where he held such a commanding lead in the final round that he started trying to beat Ben Hogan's all-time U.S. Open record of 276 for four rounds.

At the start of the final nine holes, with Palmer seven strokes ahead, his challenger Billy Casper had actually confessed out loud that he was aiming for second place. Casper, who applied an accountant's risk assessment to each shot, couldn't imagine making up the deficit.

Casper's capitulation emboldened Palmer to take risks that cost him two shots in three holes. But this did not deter him. Still focused on history rather than victory, he went for every pin and was actually annoyed to see Casper playing it safe. But instead of heroics, Palmer's adrenaline produced a cascade of bogeys. Bravado turned to desperation as every bad shot made Palmer think that he needed to recover with something extraordinary. The tournament ended in a tie. Casper, putting brilliantly, won the play-off.

As his victories became fewer each year, and his debacle at the Olympic Club settled in his mind, Palmer was forced to consider a different kind of golf. He arrived in Los Angeles for the start of the 1972 tour with his mind made up. He announced that he would adopt a lighter schedule, and a less daring approach to the game, with an eye toward winning one of the Majors. It bothered him that his last victory in one of golf's four premier events had been eight years previous. He wanted another chance to show he could do it, even if it meant altering his style. "I'm forty-two years old," he told the press in Los Angeles. "I'm not going to try to birdie the world anymore." Even a king's confidence could be shaken.

While Palmer confronted problems in his game, and perhaps the fear that his brilliance was fading, Lee Trevino faced a different challenge. Ever since he had burst onto the scene at Oak Hill, he had become the subject of ever-greater expectations and ever-more-intense scrutiny. By 1972, he was considered a contender at every tournament and a good story for every sportswriter. His mere presence improved the gate receipts for local sponsors, and the people who bought tickets expected both great golf and amusing antics from the Merry Mex.

It was hard work being so merry; harder still when the putts didn't fall. In Los Angeles, on the very first nine holes of the year, Trevino was a miserable five over par. He finished the day with a 74 and never got close to the leaders. The

$702.27 he would earn for the week hardly helped in his quest for the year's money title. Veteran George Archer would win the tournament and $30,000 in an eighteen-hole play-off against Tommy Aaron and Dave Hill.

It did not fit into Jack Nicklaus's Grand Slam plan to play at Los Angeles. He felt the time would be better spent resting and preparing for the Bing Crosby Pro–Am, which would be played the following week at three courses on the Monterey Peninsula, 120 miles south of San Francisco. One of the three courses used for the tournament–Pebble Beach Golf Links– would also be the site of the 1972 U.S. Open come June. The more time Nicklaus spent there, the better he would feel about playing that leg of the Slam. (In contrast, Trevino joked that his preparation for the U.S. Open at Pebble would include spending "a whole week beforehand resting in bed.") The highly deliberate Nicklaus arrived early enough to play three practice rounds and polish his game.

Begun in 1937 as a barbecue for Crosby, his showbiz friends, and a few pro golfers, the tournament had evolved into the ultimate expression of the golf tournament as celebrity carnival. Actors, singers, baseball players, and comics played alongside touring professionals on tough, ocean-bound golf courses that constitute the most beautiful playground on earth. By the early 1970s the Crosby–not the Masters, or the U.S. Open–had the highest TV rating of any golf broadcast. The viewers just loved watching their favorite stars hack it around.

Crosby had inspired a string of sponsorship deals connecting entertainment figures–mainly singers and comedians–

to the PGA Tour. This not-so-odd coupling reached its peak in 1972 as Dean Martin and Jackie Gleason joined Glen Campbell, Andy Williams, Bob Hope, and Danny Thomas to sponsor golf tournaments. In years to come, corporations would supplant the celebs, leaching the spice and glamour from the game. AT&T, which would take over the Pebble Beach tournament, just couldn't throw a party like Bing.

At the Crosby, all the besotted silliness—Ray Bolger drunk in the lodge, Jack Lemmon laughing on the practice green—could distract a serious pro. And things got worse as the tournament progressed. On the final day, some of the pro–am teams that had no chance to win could be counted on to become drunk and disorderly. Of course, all of the nonsense was counterbalanced by the fact that two rounds of the Crosby—including the final day's play—were conducted at venerable Pebble Beach.

Carved out of one of the most beautiful and expensive parcels of seaside property in the world, Pebble is a dramatic blend of earth, wind, and water. Holes six through eleven run along the crashing Pacific, as does the 550-yard-long finishing hole. In January, when the Crosby is played, ocean winds at Pebble can blow so hard that a wood may be needed on hole number seven, a par-three hole that juts a mere 103 yards into the sea.

Tradition calls for rain and cold, but at the 1972 edition of the Crosby warm temperatures and calm winds prevailed at midmorning, when Nicklaus stepped onto the first tee at Cypress Point. He promptly showed what all his hard work with Jack Grout had wrought. His score—66—was just one shy of the course's tournament-play record and good enough to put him three strokes ahead of Lee Trevino and two lesser-known pros named Larry Mowry and Paul Moran. Trevino seemed pleased at the end of his round, given that it was so cold and dark when he teed off at 7:24 A.M. that he could see his breath in the frosty air but had trouble following his ball.

Though early morning chills would continue, the weather got even better as the week went on. On Friday, under a sunny sky, Nicklaus gave back his lead with a front-nine 40 and a finishing score of 74 on the treacherous Spyglass Hill Golf Course. Designed by Robert Trent Jones and opened in 1966, Spyglass was the single hardest course played by the PGA Tour. The majority of players couldn't score par on this layout, which runs through sand dunes, skirts the sea, and then climbs into towering forest. (A particularly charming feature of Spyglass is the large herd of deer that feasts on the fairways and rough.) In '72, Tony Jacklin, the British truck driver's son who won the 1969 British Open and 1970 U.S. Open, was one of the few who bested this course. He shot 70 to join Nicklaus at the top of the field. Trevino was three shots behind.

As the weekend arrived, the perfect weather, the beauty of the landscape, and the insulated culture of the moneyed community that hosted the tournament all lent the affair a timeless quality. Big golf contests generally take place in this sort of cushy isolation. For four days, the competitors are the center of a world of their making. They focus on the shots they must make, their practice, and the social engagements set for most evenings. At the Crosby, Hollywood and sports celebrities gave pro golf an even stronger air of both separateness and excitement. After their rounds, players could wander into the lodge and find almost anything they wanted—food, drink, gambling, drugs, sex—in or near a suite of rooms they called the Snakepit. A nonstop card game took place in the suite, with the actors and singers generally losing plenty of cash to the golfers.

Whether you were on the course or in the Snakepit, the outside world could be ignored at Pebble Beach. In San Francisco circa 1972, there was much to be ignored. In the week of the Crosby Pro–Am, police arrested half a dozen protesters who had donned Ku Klux Klan–style robes and disrupted one of Stanford University professor William Shockley's lectures. Shockley's views on the racial inferiority of blacks were attracting frequent protests. In Berkeley, a young Alice Cooper shocked audiences with rock performances that featured a boa constrictor and sidemen in dresses. In San Jose, eighteen people were arrested at a rally in support of Angela Davis. A political activist, Davis was on trial for aiding in a murder that occurred during a prison break. She would be found not guilty.

In the Bay Area and beyond, the nation was still whirling through the social, political, and geopolitical turmoil that began in the 1960s. During the week of the 1972 Crosby tournament, Gloria Steinem was preparing the first issue of *Ms.* magazine. The drug culture still reigned in many quarters, and in Vietnam, the North launched five different small offensives against American and South Vietnamese troops.

Though they were mainly disconnected from the conflicts of the times, the pro golfers were not completely immune to social trends. Many found themselves in heated discussions about women's rights with their wives and girlfriends. Others, as Nicklaus would later confess, would indulge in marijuana. (This was hardly remarkable given that a 1972 poll found more than half of American college students had used illegal drugs.) Many players, including some married ones, enjoyed the looser mores encouraged by the sexual revolution. But very few were touched deeply by the more serious issues of the day. The issues of the civil rights movement and the Vietnam War barely crept into their lives.

One exception was Tom Weiskopf, Nicklaus's fellow Ohioan. In 1968, Weiskopf had been leading the tour's money list when his draft status was reclassified and he was summoned to the Army reserves. He missed the last third of the season and his shot at the money title while undergoing basic training at an Army camp in Louisiana. For the next five years, he would spend Sunday nights racing from tournaments, or wherever else he might be, to his Monday morning assignment as an Army clerk typist. Until 1973, he faced the threat of being called for active duty at any moment.

While Weiskopf was concerned about being called to fight, Brian "Buddy" Allin was trying to forget his experiences on the front lines. A second-year PGA Tour player, Allin was one of just two who could claim combat experience in Vietnam. (The other was a younger player named John Jacobs.) Allin had enlisted in the U.S. Army after a frustrating stint at Brigham Young University, where he had played on the golf team with future pro star Johnny Miller. He had served eighteen months as an artillery officer, directing fire at positions held by the North Vietnamese and the

Vietcong. Though very youthful looking—he had freckles and bushy hair and weighed all of 130 pounds—Allin had been an exceptionally tough soldier. He had fought mainly on the Cambodian border and had seen much more action than the average enlisted man.

When he came home from the war, Allin was twenty-five years old and torn between a return to college and taking a shot at pro golf. Noting that Miller, whom he had beaten many times in college, was doing well in pro golf, Allin chose the tour. He loaded his wife and newborn son into a brand-new, sickly green American Motors Gremlin, and went looking for tournaments. With a victory at the 1971 Greensboro Open he had earned the right to play in every event of the 1972 tournament season.

Though the PGA Tour briefly promoted Allin as a patriotic symbol, he understood the country's pain where the war was concerned and played down that aspect of his life. He preferred to focus on golf, and it seemed a bit absurd to talk about the cruel rigors of combat while wearing plaid pants and spiked golf shoes.

"Besides, we weren't exactly welcomed back with parades," recalled Allin, who would win five titles in his career. "So I kind of played that down. Pretty soon I was just able to go there and compete. I was one of the guys."

Besides the Vietnam veterans, the other group on tour who directly faced the main controversies of the day were the handful of African American competitors: Jim Dent, Charlie and Curtis Sifford, Charles Owens, Jim Thorpe, and Lee Elder. In 1972, Elder was the most visible among them. In the previous year he had risked the ire of many black Americans by accepting Gary Player's offer to play in South Africa. Together the two had broken that country's sports color barrier. On that same trip Elder had won the 1971 Nigerian Open. He came home to the United States and announced he expected an invitation to play in the Masters.

The issue of Augusta National, the Masters, and race was white-hot in 1972. From its inception in 1934, the Masters had never invited an African American player. Past champions didn't do it with the single slot they allotted, and not one, not even PGA Tour–winner Sifford, met the other criteria. This state of affairs made some people suspect that the system was rigged to keep blacks out. With its emphasis on rewarding former winners and Masters participants, the rules certainly tended to guard the status quo. But with his victory in Nigeria, Lee Elder believed the dam would be broken.

At the Crosby, Elder began with two decent rounds that put him six strokes behind the leader. Allin was one shot worse. Both survived the cut to play the weekend, for money. Allin would stumble and eventually leave town with just $280. Elder held up a little better and would take $525. These figures would seem ridiculously small a few generations later. But at a time when a decent motel room could be had for $8 and a new Toyota was less than $2,000, those checks were big enough to justify staying out on tour.

Of course, the players who began the weekend at the top of the leaderboard were not concerned with just staying on tour. They each intended to win the $28,000 first prize, and Jack Nicklaus hoped to accomplish more. He wanted to experience high-pressure rounds on the course that would host the U.S. Open. And he wanted to demonstrate to his chief rivals that he was entirely serious about the coming year and the Slam.

The Saturday morning leaderboard found Nicklaus and Jacklin chased by half a dozen others, including Trevino. SuperMex played the first sixteen holes well enough to tie the leaders. But on seventeen, a 209-yard par three, his tee shot bored into the side of a bunker, right under its grass lip. He needed two strokes just to get it out. The double bogey he scored ruined the day's work.

While many in the gallery expected Trevino to bedevil the front runners, it was young Johnny Miller who mounted the real challenge. Playing almost two hours after Nicklaus, Miller enjoyed absolutely ideal weather conditions: a seventy-degree temperature, low humidity, a slight breeze. Tony Jacklin would later say, "I never saw a more perfect day on any golf course anywhere in the world."

On this perfect day, Miller made six birdies and only one bogey. A San Francisco–area native, he benefited from having played the course many times. After the round, he admitted that over the years he had made so many birdies on number five, a pleasantly easy par three, that he simply expected one every time.

Six feet two inches tall, slim and strong, the blond-haired Miller had appeared on the tour in 1969 with the kind of grace and good looks that Jack Nicklaus had needed a diet and fashion makeover to acquire. (Occasionally Miller even worked as a fashion model.) Like Nicklaus, he had displayed remarkable talent as an amateur. The highlight of his pre-professional years came when the U.S. Open was played at San Francisco's Olympic Club in 1966. He had planned to work there as a caddie but then qualified to compete. He finished eighth. He was just nineteen years old. Big things had been expected from Miller on the pro circuit, but in the first three years of his career he had managed but one victory, the 1971 Southern Open.

Given his obvious gifts and modest performance, many touring pros questioned Miller's competitive drive. He just didn't seem hungry. But while it appeared that winning didn't mean much to him, the truth was that Miller was simply a cool player who was confident in his swing and his destiny. On Saturday at Pebble he rolled in one clutch putt after another. Save for a few drives that were nudged slightly to the right, he played flawlessly. And when he found himself in the lead at the end of the day, he sounded like an old champion rather than a one-win wonder. "I'm not shaking in my boots," he said. "They'll have to catch me."

Glorious weather, the prospects of local boy Miller, and the high standing of Nicklaus, Trevino, and Jacklin brought more than 18,000 people to Pebble Beach for the final Crosby round. Marshals struggled to keep them behind the ropes strung beside the teeing grounds and begged for quiet around the greens.

While the golf crowd in Monterey scrambled after the leaders, in millions of homes around the country, people gathered in anticipation of pro football's Super Bowl VI. (The hype around the big game had already reached Roman numeral proportions.) The Miami Dolphins would play against the Dallas Cowboys. Dallas had lost the previous year's championship 16–13, and fans expected the Cowboys to play ferociously. The game had drawn two presidents into its orbit. Richard Nixon offered advice on offense to Dolphins coach Don Shula, while Lyndon Johnson rooted for Dallas.

With the game scheduled for mid-afternoon Eastern time, the broadcast of the Crosby tournament became the background music for the pre–Super Bowl parties. (The NBC network was to air both the golf and the game.) But as the kickoff drew near, the golf tournament moved from the background to become the center of attention. The tournament had grown so dramatic that even Cowboy fans with half a six-pack already under their belts couldn't resist watching.

Although the ideal conditions appeared to demand that someone shoot a very low score, it seemed for a while that no one wanted to win it. Trevino charged at Miller with birdies on holes two, three, and four. He was actually tied for the lead as he stood in the fairway on the sixth, the first of the true ocean holes on the course. He would later explain that his right hand felt numb as he made his downswing. The result was a pushed shot that floated right, over a cliff, and onto the rocky shore of Stillwater Cove. His double bogey left the battle to Nicklaus and Miller, who were playing one hole behind.

For fifteen holes Nicklaus and Miller battled fiercely, with Miller losing the one-shot lead he had owned when he rolled out of bed. He had missed a few birdie putts but otherwise played well against an opponent who had vastly greater experience, if not a much better arsenal of shots. By this time it was after four o'clock on the East Coast, and the TV audience was growing by the minute.

On a course with so many hazards, so many cliffs, and so much ocean to contend with, the sixteenth hole is not the first place one would look to for excitement. It is a relatively mod-est, 402-yard par four that bends to the left and ends up at a green that is weakly defended by bunkers on its flanks. It may be argued that the hole offers a bit of respite before the final two. After all, seventeen is a long par three with its green set on a sliver of cliff, and eighteen requires a brave tee shot over Monterey Bay to a fairway that continues around the water to a green that's 548 yards distant.

It's possible that some part of Johnny Miller was already anticipating the test of those last two holes as he stood in the sixteenth fairway. Nicklaus had come up a little short with an eight iron. Miller had a sidehill lie, so he chose a seven and prepared to hit it hard. He made what looked like his typical smooth swing, but as soon as the club hit the ball, he, the gallery, and everyone watching on TV knew he had somehow left the face open. The result was a horrible shank—the kind hit by a thirty-handicapper—that squirted right and into the crowd.

Miller had choked. Now he had to regain his composure. Unable to reach the green from where his ball lay, he aimed for one of the guardian bunkers. He made the shot he wanted and walked up to the ball confident enough in his sand play to believe the worst he could score was a bogey. He almost made par with a blast that hit the flagstick. He walked off the green one behind his opponent, which is nothing to be ashamed of, given that he was up against Nicklaus, one-on-one, for the championship.

A bogey by Nicklaus on the seventeenth produced a deadlock at the end of the round. All over America, Checz Whiz flowed freely as football fans sat down to become golf fans and NBC extended the broadcast to show a play-off. The first man to win a hole would take the $28,000 first prize. The advantage belonged to Nicklaus. He had far more experience. And after his shank on number sixteen, Miller had approached every shot with the dreadful feeling it was going to happen again.

Hauling back to the fifteenth hole, where TV cameras were in place, Miller heard the cheers a gallery would offer a hometown David going up against the biggest giant in golf. Nicklaus couldn't help noticing that once again he was being forced into the role of the bad guy. Of course, his long experience with Palmer's Army had made him almost immune to a crowd's coldness. It only made him focus more sharply.

Besides having the crowd behind him, Miller could take comfort in the fact that he had putted better than Nicklaus all day. But in the nerve-jangling circumstances of a play-off, nothing about the previous eighteen holes matters. All that matters is getting your ball into the cup first. Miller had the chance, on the first hole, but he missed an eighteen-footer. Nicklaus followed. His ball was fifteen feet from the hole, in a spot quite near to one Miller had occupied an hour earlier. He knew the line. He knew the speed. He knew it would go in. It did. He won.

Dallas won the Super Bowl, 24–3, in one of the more boring championship games ever played.

The PGA Tour's swing through the West went from Pebble Beach to Tucson, San Diego, Honolulu, Palm Springs, and Phoenix. The competition was so fierce that play-offs were required to settle five out of the first seven tournaments of the year.

For the most part, the tour succeeded in maintaining itself as a world apart from politics and controversy. But not always. In Palm Springs, Vice President Spiro Agnew played as an amateur at the Bob Hope Desert Classic, and the tournament's organizers could not resist handing silly placards to a group of young women who then pretended to mount a protest of Agnew's appearance on the grounds that he was a bad golfer. Given that Americans had died in recent protests for civil rights, and against the Vietnam War, the spectacle of teenagers in pressed skirts conducting a mock protest for the entertainment of an all-white, mostly wealthy gallery was almost surreal. At the very least, this joke in poor taste communicated where the tour stood, politically and socially. It also suggested why many black players still felt uncomfortable on tour.

Despite the black players' feelings of unease, one of the more remarkable sidelights of the early season was the strong play of these professionals, who competed on the tour in far greater numbers in 1972 than at any other time. Each one had played his way onto the tour when the prohibition against blacks in the PGA was finally dropped in 1961, and golf became the last big-time sport to integrate.

Nearly all the black players had come from the caddie ranks and had competed on the United Golf Association (UGA) tour, a circuit of tournaments for African Americans that for years had offered them the only opportunity to play pro events. The purses were abysmal–$800 for first place was typical in the mid-1960s. And the host courses were rarely top quality. As talented as they were, the players of the UGA had limited experience on more demanding courses. As a result, when they finally made it to the PGA Tour, they had to make up for huge gaps in experience.

Newcomers are most likely to fall victim to their inexperience when they climb to the top of the leaderboard. This was demonstrated early in the 1972 season. Charles Owens, a rookie, grabbed national headlines when he dominated the first day of play at the Dean Martin–Tucson Open with a score of 65. Owens attracted attention wherever he played because he held the club cross-handed and walked the course with a limp caused by an injury he had suffered during his training as an Army paratrooper for the Korean War. Owens had shattered his knee when the pilot of the plane he jumped from missed a landing area and instead dumped Owens and his fellow troopers into a Louisiana swamp.

Physical disability was just one of the obstacles Owens had overcome to play on the pro tour. As a greenkeeper's son, he had been raised in a family of ten that occupied a shack beside the ninth green at the Winter Haven (Florida) Golf Club. He taught himself a cross-handed swing by hitting bottle caps down a dirt road with sticks. Later, he made his own clubs by attaching homemade wooden shafts to the heads of clubs that temperamental players had snapped in half and discarded. In the long twilight of summer he and his brother would sneak onto the course and swing away until their mother called them home or the local sheriff ran them into the orange groves. Later, in the service, he was denied a chance to play in the kind of Army-sponsored tournaments in which Lee Trevino had received so much of his competitive experience. The contests may have been open to talented Mexican Americans, but blacks were not welcome.

Despite being barred from many courses and whites-only tournaments, despite his injury and his self-taught, cross-handed swing, Charles Owens had made it through the PGA Tour qualifying tournament and earned the right to play on the tour. At Tucson the crowd had marveled at his drives—he could smash the ball 325 yards—and his unconventional swing. "It drove the establishment crazy," he would later say about his method, "because it proved that the important thing was getting the ball in the hole, and that any good athlete could do it."

In his first round at Tucson, Owens had teed off at 10:30 in the morning, in pleasantly warm conditions. He hit his drive, then an eight iron for an easy birdie three on the first hole. He went on to reach almost every green in regulation and he putted flawlessly. His score was his lowest so far on the PGA Tour, and the gallery he attracted was the biggest he had ever played before.

On the next day, Owens teed off at 7:15 A.M. in weather so cold that he wore two sweaters and a shirt to keep from freezing. This time he hit his driver and a two iron on the first hole, made bogey, and never felt comfortable. He struggled to a 77 and fell from contention. But for a moment, the surprising Owens had been the hottest player on tour.

Along with Charlie Owens's one great round, the West Coast swing offered other pleasant surprises and diversions from the main story line propelled by Nicklaus, Trevino, and Palmer. Among the winners of the early season were two old-timers. The first was Paul Harney, a long-hitting club pro from Massachusetts who appeared on tour every winter while his home course was under snow, and then went home after the Masters. A silver-haired forty-two-year-old, Harney overtook young Hale Irwin's three-shot lead on the final nine holes to win the Andy Williams–San Diego Open. Two weeks later Bob Rosburg, who at forty-five was three years older than Arnold Palmer, beat three rising stars named Johnny Miller, Jerry Heard, and Lanny Wadkins to win the Bob Hope Desert Classic.

As the tour moved east, neither Nicklaus nor Trevino was in the top five on the money list. After winning $28,000 at Pebble, Nicklaus had collected only $3,793 more out West, enough for sixth on the money list. Trevino was roughly $10,000 behind him, in tenth place.

While anyone else would be happy with tenth place on the PGA Tour, the numbers were deceiving. Hell-bent for the money title, Trevino had pushed himself hard, playing six out of seven tournaments, traveling more than 12,000 miles to do it. Between practicing and the demands of outside businesses, it was a punishing schedule. He had averaged only $3,500 in winnings per week. At that rate, he would never take the year's money title.

In contrast, Nicklaus had chosen to rest instead of playing

Los Angeles, Tucson, and Phoenix. Of the four tournaments he did play, he won one and finished tenth in another. His earnings were more than $8,000 per week, and he hadn't stressed his body or his mind. He was keeping to his own Grand Slam schedule.

Like Nicklaus, Arnold Palmer had taken it easy, playing just four times. But his best finish was sixth at the Hope Classic, and his total earnings on the coast were just $10,813. If this was the new Arnie, then his quest for another Major was a long shot at best.

CHAPTER 2

When Jack Nicklaus plays well, he wins.
When he plays badly, he finishes second.
When he plays terribly, he finishes third.
                                              —Johnny Miller

As the 1972 PGA Tour left Phoenix, its immediate destination was Florida, where four tournaments would be played. Augusta, six weeks further down the road, already whispered for attention. Fame and history waited at the first Major, the first test of Nicklaus's Grand Slam odyssey, the first Masters to be played after the passing of Bobby Jones.

Of course, money talks in more than a whisper, and the huge first prize at the Jackie Gleason–Inverrary Classic in Fort Lauderdale was loud enough to overwhelm any distractions. In 1972 the $52,000 winner's check at Inverrary was the biggest prize ever offered by a golf tournament. (Some perspective is gained when you consider that at the time the annual median *family* income was $10,120. And the average baseball player in 1972 made $31,000 for an entire season's work.) The Gleason tournament was so rich that second place—almost $30,000—equaled the champion's prize at the U.S. Open. All this cash meant that when the tournament began, all the big names—Nicklaus, Trevino, Palmer, and Player—would share the same green acreage for the first time that year.

Gary Player arrived in Florida after playing well in tournaments on three continents. His insistence on competing in Africa, Asia, and Europe allowed him fewer than twenty appearances per year in the United States. This schedule was a bit of a handicap when it came to his standing on the American tour. He could not expect to win the money title, for example, because he just didn't play in enough tournaments. An almost puritanical lifestyle—rigorous diet, daily exercise, rigid sleep schedule—helped Player compensate for the stress of travel and made him the most well-conditioned athlete in golf. Built like a swimmer, with strong arms and a narrow waist, he never seemed to show an ounce of fat. This, combined with the fact that he was always tanned and impeccably dressed, meant he could pass as a film or TV star. During one appearance on Perry Como's TV variety show, Player came across so well that afterward he was contacted by Hollywood agents who wanted him to do a screen test.

As much as his global travel placed added demands on Player, an even greater burden came from the mere fact that he was a prominent South African who had refused to turn his back on his country. From the start of his pro career he was confronted with questions about his homeland's racial problems. In 1961, at the age of twenty-five, Player had struggled to answer *Sports Illustrated* on the issue of apartheid. His reply, which reflected mainstream white opinion in South Africa at the time, would later seem racist and closed-minded.

"Any government that is elected by the people of South Africa will do its best for the entire country," he said, not mentioning the fact that blacks couldn't vote. "And with the white people in our country in such a minority, you couldn't do very well to give the blacks complete freedom and power. All you have to do is look at the trouble in the Congo to realize it wouldn't be long before the blacks would chop off all our heads."

Although he had defended apartheid in the late 1950s and early 1960s, Player had undergone such a substantial change of heart and mind that by the late 1960s he was an active advocate for integration, especially in sports. "I realized that I had been brainwashed, like everybody else, to accept the system as it was," Player recalled decades later. As a boy, after his mother fell sick with cancer and died, Player was raised in part by a black man hired to care for him after school. He loved this man deeply, and yet never questioned the punishing social structure that relegated him to second-class status. This view began to change when, at seventeen, Player began to travel the globe to play golf.

"I got out in the world and came to understand our country was wrong. We were jailing people like Nelson Mandela who we knew we would have to deal with someday when real change came. I knew that."

In America, the change in Player's position on apartheid was not well understood. Many, including members of the radical Black Panther Party, continued to view him as a symbol of racism and cited his early comments as evidence. Others took issue with Player being allowed to compete in America while Arthur Ashe, the great black tennis player, was barred from playing in South Africa. Together these two groups mounted protests at many of Player's appearances in America.

The worst incident came at the 1969 PGA Championship, where nine people were arrested for disrupting Player's performance. Along with cheering his errors and shouting during his backswing, the protesters hurled cups filled with soft drinks at Player and at one point even rushed at him on a putting green. Nicklaus was with Player on the green and raised his putter in self-defense as the protesters were blocked by security men.

Away from the golf course, Player was verbally abused in public places, and there were times when one crank call after another would be made to the hotel rooms or private homes where he stayed during tournaments. He had trouble ignoring these contacts and often tried to respond to them, hoping to clarify his stand on apartheid and challenge his critics. He rarely succeeded.

Though these incidents were upsetting, Player was just as galled by the fact that American pros were able to coast along in the isolation of the PGA Tour and never deal with their own country's problems. "In that time period America's inner cities were being burned, students were being shot on college campuses, but none of the American players had to talk about that," said Player. "It was okay to confront me, but I guess might was right where America was concerned."

Forced to be a character in his country's racial drama, Player cultivated contacts with both the ruling whites and the leaders of the black population. As his career wore on, he accumulated enormous popularity as his country's top athlete. He used his position to promote racial change. During the 1970 golf season he published a column in *The Sunday Tribune* of Johannesburg calling for the integration of sports in his country. In 1971, he pushed matters a bit harder. As the season ended, Player approached his friend Lee Elder with an idea. Player wanted him to come to South Africa to play in a national tournament and stage an exhibition in Swaziland, one of the semiautonomous black homelands in South Africa. This was no small matter. South Africa had never allowed whites and blacks to compete in sport. Elder and Player would be the first.

Elder was one of the best-known and most talented African American pros. After years of scraping by as a hustler and champion of blacks-only tournaments, Elder had played his way onto the PGA Tour in 1967. In his first year he almost beat Jack Nicklaus at the formidable Firestone Country Club in Akron. The two played a five-hole play-off in the American Golf Classic. Elder and Nicklaus both had birdie putts on the final hole. Though Nicklaus made his and Elder missed, he established himself as a gifted player. Nevertheless, he would have to endure threats and shouts of "boy" and "nigger" from galleries throughout his career.

Racial pressure was also focused on Elder from within the black community, where many people regarded golf as a white man's domain and suspected that he had tried too hard to get along within the game. Accepting an offer to join Player in South Africa would only serve to make Elder more vulnerable to these critics. But Elder was a disciple of Martin Luther

King, Jr., and one of the defining experiences of his life had been the 1963 march on Washington, which he had joined. He witnessed King's famous "I Have a Dream" speech on the Mall in Washington. He believed in peacemaking and would accept Player's offer, if certain conditions were met. The galleries could not be segregated, and Elder would be free to visit any part of the country and to use every public facility—hotels, restaurants, rest rooms—everything.

This freedom was actually more than Elder had experienced in the United States during much of his life. As a boy in Dallas he had caddied at Glen Lakes, alongside Lee Trevino, but had to take a streetcar across town to find a course where blacks were allowed to play. Until the early 1960s, the PGA tour had a whites-only policy, and Elder had to be content with a little hustling and dominating the tournaments of the United Golf Association, the black tour. He made the PGA Tour in 1967, but right up to the 1970s, Elder had been denied access to the clubhouse when the tour played in Pensacola.

Elder's conditions were no different from what Player would have proposed himself. Shortly after he arrived home from America, Player went to Cape Town to meet with Prime Minister John Vorster. Though a staunch supporter of apartheid, Vorster was interested in presenting a softer image of South Africa to the outside world. He sat stern-faced as Player outlined his request. When Player finished, Vorster sat silent for a long moment and then said, simply, "Go ahead."

In November of 1971, while other American golf pros vacationed and practiced, Elder and Player competed before mixed-race crowds that swelled to 10,000. Black South

Africans were delighted to see that a black man could match the great Gary Player on the course. Elder overheard two women who were watching from behind a fence at the club laugh as one said, "That's why they created apartheid here, because they knew that blacks could play better than whites."

Vorster was good to his word, and Elder traveled without limitations. However, the prime minister was incapable of shaking his visitor's hand. At a reception, he turned and walked away as Elder approached. And though Player had insisted that Vorster greet Elder at some point during the trip, the best Vorster could muster was a blunt phone call placed to Elder's room at the Johannesburg Holiday Inn.

Elder topped his African trip with his win at the Nigerian Open against a field that included eight members of the British Ryder Cup team. As champion of a foreign open, he promptly announced that he expected an invitation to the Masters, which no black man had ever played. The convoluted rules of the Masters allowed for champions of foreign nations to be invited, but not if they were Americans who had won abroad. Elder was not invited.

Though the racial deadlock at the Masters remained, Elder and Player had nevertheless achieved something far more significant in smashing the race barrier in South African sports. When Player came back to the United States in 1972, he eagerly anticipated a reunion with Elder and a return to top-flight competition. The Fort Lauderdale tournament would start a long stretch of events that would carry him through Augusta and the rest of the Majors.

For Jack Nicklaus, the tough group of competitors who would play in Fort Lauderdale provided a well-timed warm-up for the Masters. The big galleries—80,000 people would attend the tournament—and more intense competition made the atmosphere close to the mood of a Major. He couldn't help but mention, however, that the lure of a $52,000 prize would benefit him, and a few others, who had long experience with high-stakes games. "The bigger the title, or the money, the easier it is to win," he said with characteristic confidence.

In contrast, both Arnold Palmer and Lee Trevino arrived in Florida with their games sputtering and in need of repair. Once a superb clutch putter, Palmer had become shaky on the greens. He had also lost his timing with the driver. For months he had been hitting one left, one right, then one straight. Bursitis made his hip hurt, and practice was difficult.

While Palmer limped around, the victim of age, Trevino flew into Fort Lauderdale carrying the heavy weight of his newly increased celebrity. The Bayer company had hired him to do a couple of aspirin commercials in Spanish. Filming was a week away, and Trevino, whose command of the language was hardly perfect, was struggling to get his lines down. He was also busy promoting golf clubs, clothing, and cars.

Trevino laughed a bit at the suggestion that he was overextending himself. "People keep knocking on my door with handsful of money," he said. "What am I going to do, tell them to go next door to Arnold Palmer or Jack Nicklaus?" Still, the stress seemed to affect his golf. His drives, normally among the straightest on tour, were as wild as Palmer's. His putting, the part of the game that is most dependent on nerves, was weak.

Nothing got better for either of them on the first day at Inverrary. Palmer put himself in bad positions off the tee and finished with a 74. Trevino could have used some aspirin himself as he struggled to a 76. After finishing his round, he stopped to jaw with the sportswriters and joked that he might have preferred to accompany President Nixon on his trip to China—Nixon was on his historic mission at the time—but practicing on the Great Wall would require some straight hitting, and that would be hard for him to do. Trevino then walked straight to the practice green and stayed there, rolling one putt after another while other players came, worked a bit, and then departed. When the sun set he was still there, alone.

As he labored in the gloom, Trevino could take some comfort in the two bogeys that Nicklaus suffered on his first two holes, and his final score of 73. Player's 72 was more respectable, but a far cry from the scorching 65 fired by Gene Littler.

Soft-spoken and blessed with a fluid swing, Littler was one of the best-liked players on tour. In eighteen years he had won twenty tournaments but only one Major, the 1961 U.S. Open. He often wondered if he might have done better in those high-stakes events if he had had a little more of the killer instinct.

Littler was tough enough to hang on to the lead through Friday. He was joined at the top by Buddy Allin, the Vietnam artillery vet, who conquered the course with a 66. As so often happens in golf, Allin's terrific performance came as a complete surprise, especially to him.

In practice rounds before the tournament started, Allin had hit the ball so poorly that he had considered withdrawing from the field, packing his wife and child into his Gremlin, and heading down the road. But before he withdrew, he went to the Inverrary practice range and spent about $30 on $2 baskets of practice balls.

Standing on the range, Allin's former college teammate Johnny Miller could see exactly what was wrong with Allin's swing. In the locker room he found Allin and offered a diagnosis: "You're picking it up on the way back." In golfer's shorthand, Miller had said that Allin was using his hands and wrists to move the club, rather than turning his body. It was an old, bad habit, and Allin knew Miller was right. One more basket of balls and he was cured. The next day he hit the ball square enough to make a 71. On Friday he used a new putter, a heavy model endorsed by Jerry Barber that he had gotten for free, to roll in a bunch of long putts and post his 66.

Allin would need a whole lot of hot putting if he was ever going to contend in a tournament. Given his size, he was hard-pressed to drive the ball more than 240 yards. In another era, when golf courses were 6,000 yards long, this would have been no problem. But Nicklaus, Palmer, and other practitioners of power golf had forced architects and superintendents to add length to their layouts. By 1972, most of the courses where the tour stopped measured over 6,800 yards, and many exceeded 7,000.

"It was hard because someone like Nicklaus just hit it so high and so far," said Allin. He tried to make up for his lack of power off the tee with better long irons and fairway woods. He could nestle a five wood onto the smallest green, and when his putter was working, he could compete with players who smashed the ball farther on every shot.

But though he would scrap his way to some victories in his short career, Allin, like many others, existed just outside the orbit of the stars. Realistic, and remarkably humble for a pro athlete, he didn't consider himself on their level. But he was close enough to see every color of the light they shed.

"Everyone had their different style," he recalled. "Jack was very nice, very calm, but he was totally focused. He just knew he was going to beat you. Arnold was different. The first time I played with Arnold, he came over to me with that look he has, shook my hand, and said, 'You get any last night?' It was like he was saying, 'Of course I did. I'm the man.'" With Trevino, Allin recalls, the mind games were more subtle, and a lot more amusing.

"He once told me and Jerry Heard that he had found the secret to the swing. 'You can never have your hands too high,' he said. I took it very seriously. Tried what he said, and it messed me up. Then the next week there'd be some other swing secret he'd tell us. We'd go off and try that too and get messed up some more."

If a star's gamesmanship wasn't enough to give him an edge, the gallery was likely to provide it for him. Allin and every other mid-level player knew that in a tight situation, Palmer, Nicklaus, Trevino, and Player could count on the fans standing behind a green to let themselves be hit by a ball that might fly well past the putting surface. This was a great advantage on long shots that were especially hard to stop on the green. Volunteers in Arnie's Army would even jump to get in front of a shot. "We all understood it," said Allin. "It was Arnold Palmer. These guys were like gods to some people."

Just the idea of facing off against the gods could rattle a young, mid-ranked pro, so it was no surprise when Buddy Allin stumbled to a 75 on Saturday. Gene Littler fell even harder, with a 77. At his age, Littler wasn't a victim of nerves. But he just didn't feel quite himself.

Among the deities, only Player and Nicklaus managed to put on a rush toward the top. Palmer recorded one of his worst scores in three years, an 80, in a round that saw him lose his composure on the tenth hole. He found a bunker on his second shot and wound up throwing his club after mishitting his sand wedge. The best his caddie Creamy Carolan could say when it was over was that perhaps one miserable round was better than a dozen middling scores. "I'm hurting, mentally," confessed Palmer.

"Jack's Hungry" read the headline in Sunday morning's *Miami Herald*. With a performance he described as "terrible," Nicklaus had nevertheless climbed to within two shots of the leaders, Gary Player and Tom Weiskopf. The sports editors understood Nicklaus and his abilities. They could be certain that he would mount a real challenge, and was likely to win.

It was Nicklaus's temperament that made the difference in a situation like this one. Everyone on tour had the ability to stick the ball within a few yards of the pin with a wedge. Everyone was capable of making a straight drive and sinking a five-foot putt. But Jack Nicklaus could make these shots, and more difficult ones, with huge amounts of money on the line, a lifetime of dreams in his heart, and what seemed like the whole world watching. Nicklaus discovered he had this grace under stress at a young age, and it gave him enormous confidence. It also had a corrosive effect on most other players. With anyone else chasing them, they could hope for a mistake.

When it was Nicklaus, they lost that hope and felt an even greater burden to play flawless golf themselves.

Flawless golf was too much to ask of Gary Player, who had at last begun to feel the effects of the demands he had placed on his well-tuned body. He would record a 74 and fall out of contention, though his final position would still be way ahead of Trevino and far better than Palmer's. Though he had bravely set his sights on breaking par after his miserable 80 on Saturday, Palmer shot a 79 on Sunday. He would finish next to last, sending a chill through the ranks of his army.

So it would be up to Weiskopf, who had been awed by Jack Nicklaus at the U.S. Open a decade earlier, to stop his hero, his role model, the man he had come to count as a friend and a mentor. "My goal was not the money, it was to beat Jack Nicklaus," he would recall. "That's how you win, not by focusing on the money, but with the same attitude you had when you were a kid playing with your friends, and all you wanted was to win."

Nicklaus and Weiskopf had become friendly enough to go hunting together in the off-season. In November 1971, they had chased elk in the wilds of New Mexico, and Weiskopf, a more gifted outdoorsman, had been amused to confront Nicklaus in an arena other than golf. While every other hunter in the group had taken an elk, Nicklaus had seen his shots miss their marks. Suspecting that the sight on Nicklaus's new rifle was misaligned, Weiskopf took him to a shooting range.

Knowing that Nicklaus would rise to any competitive opportunity, Weiskopf suggested a little target practice after the gun was fixed. He squeezed off a shot that hit the bull's-eye on a target that was a good three iron away. It made a hole the diameter of a dime as it bored through the target. While Nicklaus was still admiring the shot, Weiskopf promptly fired a second. Nicklaus raised binoculars to his eyes.

"I can't see it," said Nicklaus.

"That's 'cause it went in the same hole."

"Damn!"

Weiskopf let Nicklaus stand there flabbergasted for a long minute before he burst into laughter and confessed to an old marksman's trick. He had fired the second shot so high it never hit the target at all. But his confidence had made Nicklaus believe he could hit a bullet hole from 200 yards.

Though no one was ever as self-assured as Jack Nicklaus on the golf course, Tom Weiskopf had the strength of his own experience to draw upon. Four years earlier, at another tournament in Florida, he had gotten so pumped up that he gave away a victory by overshooting the final green and making a double bogey. He had learned then that adrenaline could be an enemy late in an exciting match. Ever since, he often compensated by using a lesser club in high-stress moments.

It was obvious to the rest of the PGA Tour that Weiskopf was the type to pump a little extra hormone in a tight situation. Weiskopf's temper was on display almost every week. But his flashes of anger were directed almost entirely at himself. He had very high standards for his performance and felt a sense of guilt, or perhaps shame, whenever he failed.

Ironically, Weiskopf was not, at heart, a cutthroat competitor. It took another hothead, Tommy Bolt, to see this. For much of his career, club-throwing "Thunder" Bolt was

the most volcanic player in golf. One story, probably apoc-
ryphal, has Bolt asking his caddie which club to use and hearing the reply, "A five, 'cause it's all we got left."

On the first day of the Gleason tournament, the fifty-four-
year-old Bolt had stumbled to a 42 on the first nine holes and,
in disgust, decided to withdraw. He ran into Weiskopf in the
clubhouse parking lot and decided to display a less-well-known
side of his personality: kindness.

"You've got the greatest swing in the world and all the
potential," he told Weiskopf in all seriousness. "But you got
to be mean. You've got to grind 'em down to win out there."
Bolt was saying that there was a difference between a blazing
temper and competitive toughness. Temper tantrums wreck
your round. Channeled aggression produces victory. Weiskopf went out with the last group to play on Sunday determined to perform with a higher level of intensity.

Playing three groups ahead of Weiskopf that day, Nicklaus was able to slip into a calm but focused state of mind
without any real effort. It was entirely natural for him to sum-
mon up his best game in tense situations, and it appeared on
the very first hole as he made a smooth five-footer for birdie.
He did the same on number two, and almost put a bunker
shot into the hole for eagle on the monstrous 578-yard third.
His tap-in for birdie there put him in first place, alone, before
Weiskopf had even hit his first drive.

Six feet four inches tall, the curly-haired Weiskopf appeared for his round sporting bushy sideburns and flared golf
pants, a nod to the fashion of the times. The scoreboard
showed the Nicklaus surge, and Weiskopf showed he was rattled by promptly making bogeys on the first two holes. Then

just as suddenly, he turned his performance around. He made three long putts, and three birdies, in a row and rolled in a nine-footer to finish the front with a score of 33.

Up ahead of Weiskopf, Nicklaus was feeling snugly comfortable in the midst of the battle. He finished with a 67, which could have easily been a 66 but for one small lapse in concentration. It had come on the sixteenth hole. Nicklaus had a two-footer for par and he pushed it, like a weekend hacker, and had to settle for a bogey. Nevertheless, as he signed his scorecard, Nicklaus was one stroke ahead of his friend and off-season hunting companion.

Behind Nicklaus, Weiskopf made his own run of birdies and recaptured the lead. He came to the seventeenth hole two shots ahead. A par and a bogey would win it. Then came a moment in the tournament that showed the huge gap between a player's experience and how it is perceived by the gallery and TV audience.

A pushed drive landed Weiskopf's ball in the right-hand rough. It was thick but not too long, and he felt comfortable swinging an iron for the green, which was less than one hundred yards away. But before settling over the ball, Weiskopf decided to pace off the yardage. He walked toward the green, counting his steps. On the way back he noticed that he had stepped in a bunker and left some footprints in the sand. He reflexively grabbed a rake and smoothed them.

By the time Weiskopf got back to his ball, the TV commentators were declaring he had made an awful blunder. The rules prohibit a player from doing anything to a bunker prior to hitting his ball out of it. Now, if Weiskopf somehow chunked his next shot into the sand, he would suffer an automatic two-stroke penalty. But a miss that would send the ball into the sand was so far from Weiskopf's mind that he would later wonder what all the fuss was about. He raked the bunker because he *knew* he was going to land the ball on the green. And he did. His thirty-foot putt followed a perfect line to the hole. The ball caught the back of the cup, popped up, and fell in with a hollow rattle.

Determined that he wouldn't let the excitement cause him to overpower his shots, Weiskopf left his driver in his golf bag and played a safe one iron off the eighteenth tee. He put his second shot in the sand, barely got the ball onto the green in three, and two-putted for bogey. He had held on, against Nicklaus, his nerves, and the fates, to win the biggest check ever handed out at a golf tournament.

Weiskopf wasn't the only one to leave Fort Lauderdale with a big grin on his face. On the last day of play, Buddy Allin recovered his composure and shot a bogey-free 69. He finished just four strokes behind the winner and three off of Nicklaus. His share of fourth place was worth $10,000, enough to buy four new Gremlins. He wouldn't get all the money, though. Like many mid-level players, Allin had a wealthy sponsor who backed him in return for splitting every prize check. He had started the year with $20,000 worth of this man's cash, which he had to repay. From that point on, he got to keep half of everything he won. Still, it was a great week for him, one of the best he would have in his seven-year career.

As Jack Nicklaus left Fort Lauderdale with his second-place check, he told the gang of sportswriters in the press tent that he had felt an extraordinary level of concentration on the course that day. "I call it making my body do what my mind wants it to do," he explained. For a man with his eye on the Majors to come, that feeling was the best trophy he could imagine.

Getting the body to do what the mind imagines is the essence of golf. It is the main difference between a game that involves a ball lying still on the ground and more active sports—baseball, basketball, hockey, and so on—that sweep mind and body into constant action and reaction. In all those other sports, there is no time to engage the brain in some sort of narrative or analysis. In fact, in most sports it's better that you not think much at all but merely allow your body to react. In golf, the time spent walking from shot to shot offers too many opportunities for worry and doubt. The swing itself begins with a quiet moment over the ball and a slow, purposeful backswing. There's plenty of time there to think about the water on the left, the trees on the right, and the putt you missed on the last green.

Whether it was deliberate or not, Lee Trevino dealt with his mind by keeping it so busy with idle chatter and jokes that there was no room for negative thoughts. Nicklaus had gone a step further. Instead of trying to blot out the negative, he cultivated the positive. During the long time he took to prepare to swing—and it was longer than most players required—Nicklaus tried to conjure a series of images in his mind, a moving picture really, of the perfectly executed shot. He wouldn't play until he had this image in his mind, and it obviously worked.

Years, perhaps decades after Nicklaus had dreamed up his method, sports psychologists discovered that successful athletes often used this technique, which was dubbed visualization. It is a technique best used in quieter moments—prior to a foul shot in basketball or a field goal attempt in football—and it works.

At Fort Lauderdale, Jack Nicklaus put the PGA Tour on notice that his body was perfectly attuned to the glorious images that played in his head. Nicklaus won the very next tournament, the Doral–Eastern Open in Miami, and in the process edged past Arnold Palmer in lifetime earnings—$1,471,000 to $1,447,000.

Nicklaus's achievement overshadowed the resurgence of Lee Trevino, who had finally begun to play well. Prior to the start of the tournament, Trevino had hidden out on the putting green at a municipal course in Miami Springs. He claimed to have hit a thousand practice putts. The hard work paid off as he shot a pair of 69s to grab the lead on Saturday morning. A rain-out on Saturday forced thirty-six holes of play on Sunday. Trevino was tied for first with Nicklaus after the first eighteen, but stopped making birdies. His even-par score allowed Nicklaus to prevail in the last round, but Trevino had regained confidence in his game. Of course, in the three remaining weeks before the Masters he would still have to deal with press and fans asking him why he was going to Augusta at all. Once again he was under extra pressure that had nothing to do with his performance on a golf course.

———

The story of Trevino and the Masters illustrates perfectly the problems that dogged the tournament at the time. The Masters was synonymous with the Old South and everything that was good and bad about it. Devotees loved the course, the old-fashioned manners of the staff, and the exclusivity of Augusta National and its tournament.

Many of those who didn't like the club and its tournament suspected its organizers of racism. No wonder. For years the club itself was a living museum of America's historic racial divide. The members behaved like blue-blazered fraternity boys at an exclusive college, polishing a veneer of gentility while privately indulging in the most base activities. In their not-so-ancient past their parties included the so-called *battle royals* conducted during tournament week. While white men in coats and ties puffed cigars and sipped whiskey, a group of young black men—about half a dozen—were herded into a boxing ring in the ballroom of a downtown hotel. They were blindfolded and then jeered and cheered as they flailed at each other until just one remained standing. Though it has been described elsewhere in matter-of-fact terms, the brutal humiliation of the *battle royal* is brilliantly evoked in Ralph Ellison's novel *Invisible Man*, which includes a stomach-souring account of these brawls.

Though the modern Masters tournament did not feature attractions like the *battle royal*, the flavor of racism was evident in the caddie corps, which was exclusively black and served a field of players that was exclusively white. One excuse made for the policy restricting the caddie jobs to blacks was that the practice preserved jobs for local men who needed the money. The trouble with this argument was that some of the caddies at the Masters were imported professionals. For example, the man who carried Jack Nicklaus's bag, Willie Petersen, came from Harlem and usually worked at a course in New Jersey.

Though the caddies drew comparatively little attention, as pro golf began to become integrated the fact that no black man had ever swung a club in the Masters tournament became a problem for many. When Charlie Sifford became the first black man to win a top-level PGA Tour event—the 1967 Greater Hartford Open—many in the press and public had clamored for him to be invited. But the tournament's Byzantine policies kept him out.

The tournament's rules limited the Masters field to about eighty players, who were invited only if they met certain criteria. For much of the tournament's history these included all former Masters winners, the top twenty-four from the previous year's tournament, players who finished high in the U.S. Open and PGA championships, British and American amateur champs, and champions of foreign nations. Up until 1971, one slot was reserved for a player who couldn't meet one of these criteria, and it was handed out by a vote of former Masters winners. This small opening for a wild-card entrant was closed in 1971 when the top eight on the PGA Tour money list were added.

By 1972, there seemed to be a sincere desire, even among some in Augusta, to have the race barrier broken. But it didn't

help that in 1971, tournament chairman Clifford Roberts described black players as "dark complected boys." In the same
year the club decided to change the invitation policy to eliminate the one slot awarded by a vote of former champions.
This happened as Gary Player was beginning a campaign to
win that spot for Elder. Finally, there was the matter of the
caddies. Roberts still insisted that only blacks carry the competitors' golf bags. The visual imagery, at a time when the
entire nation was concerned about race relations, was too
much for critics to take.

Besides race, some players were rubbed the wrong way
by the club's rigid rules, and the way they were imposed by
the dictatorial tournament chairman. Decorum, as the club
defined it, was of the highest value. Like schoolmarms in
men's trousers, scolding officials at Augusta policed everything
players did and said, and were likely to demand a player apologize for raising his voice or uttering a four-letter word. Paul
Harney, who played very well at Augusta, felt that the mood
of the place was overhyped and overstarched, and that the
way the players and the press quaked in fear of Roberts was
ridiculous.

Like Harney, Lee Trevino was annoyed by the over-
managed quality of the Masters tournament. No other event
placed such rigid controls on the movements and activities of
players. But more important, Trevino just didn't like the golf
course. He felt it was designed specifically for long hitters, like
Nicklaus, and players who could comfortably draw the ball
right to left. (Trevino played a left-to-right fade.) Shorter drivers found themselves firing into the sides of hills that the
power players could clear. He also believed that the absence

of rough on the course meant there was no premium on accuracy. Overall, few golf courses offered more to the big bombers and less to the creative little guy.

Trevino expressed his unfiltered opinions on Augusta National in a locker-room conversation he had with Charlie Sifford in 1969. Sifford had started off their chat with complaints about the fact that the former Masters champions had never used their votes to invite a black man to the club. Trevino had responded by saying, essentially, the Masters ain't so great anyway. A reporter who overheard all this published what Trevino said. After that, Trevino turned down invitations to play in Augusta in 1970 and 1971. Both years he spent Masters week playing in the New Mexico PGA Spring Championship.

Finally, in the winter of 1971, Jack Nicklaus took Trevino aside after the two of them played a charity event at the Breakers in West Palm Beach. He urged Trevino to reconsider the Masters and argued with him about the golf course and the game. "You can win anywhere," he insisted. Trevino listened, and decided to try Augusta again. But he knew that the press, and the people who loved the Masters, would be watching him intently.

Gary Player felt little discomfort about Augusta National. After all, he had won there in 1969. He was looking forward to another try and gearing up his game. The results of his practice showed at the New Orleans Open, two weeks before the Masters.

Player opened the tournament with a lackluster 73. The

gallery and sportswriters kept their focus on a lovely duel between Nicklaus and Billy Casper. The two tied for first at the end of the first round, and Casper took a two-stroke lead after the second. He did this with brilliant putting—he was perhaps the best putter on tour—even as Nicklaus outdrove him by as much as fifty yards on every one of the par fours and par fives. It was a remarkable performance by Casper, especially considering that he had taken a month away from golf prior to coming to New Orleans.

As play began on the final day in New Orleans, the question seemed to be whether Casper could continue to putt well enough to stave off Nicklaus. Few of those who cruised down General de Gaulle Drive to the Lakewood Country Club had any thought that Gary Player might win. But Player felt it was possible, and it was likely that Nicklaus felt it, too. Nicklaus never counted Player out.

After three straight days of perfect warm, dry weather, Sunday brought clouds, cold, and wind that seemed to rust Billy Casper's touch on the greens. A few misses and he was on his way to a ruinous 76. Nicklaus was taken out by a double bogey on the eighth hole, which seemed to drain his enthusiasm. It would be left for Player, clad head to toe in black, to seize the prize. The turning point came on the fifteenth hole when he removed his shoes and socks and used a wedge to splash his ball out of the shallows of a pond and save par. He would roll in the winning putt on eighteen and pump his fist in victory.

Arnold Palmer was still struggling. Unlike Nicklaus, who went early to Augusta to practice, Palmer chose to compete in the Greater Greensboro Open. He played well, reaching the final day in a good position to win. But anyone who looked closely could see that he wasn't happy. As he played, the grimaces outnumbered the smiles, and his bad shots seemed to be getting the best of him.

On Sunday at Greensboro, Palmer's playing partners had to duck when he flung his putter in disgust after missing a short putt on the fourteenth green. Even for a fiery competitor like Palmer, it was an excessive display of temper. He held a two-stroke lead and was atop the scoreboard for the first time all year. He should have been in a positive frame of mind.

On the sixteenth hole, still burning with frustration, Palmer lost his focus and hit his tee shot into a creek. After a visit to a greenside bunker and a missed eight-foot putt, he made triple bogey and the championship was lost. Though he finished just two shots short of victory and played his best golf of the year by far, it wasn't at all clear that he was mentally ready for the Masters.

Gary Player had his own mental lapses at Greensboro. He was disqualified for absentmindedly failing to sign his scorecard after the third round. He had been just one shot off the lead at the time.

For his part, Trevino was still drinking hard, practicing too little, and distracted by business deals and sponsors' demands. Given that he didn't much like Augusta anyway, he was not looking forward to the Masters at all.

But no matter how they felt about their games, or the aura

of the Masters, every player who packed his bags for Augusta could be grateful that he wasn't Gene Littler. After struggling to make the cut at Doral, Littler had gone home to La Jolla, California, for some rest. Days after he arrived, he went to his family physician for a routine physical and pointed to a hard little lump in his left arm that he called "a little piece of gristle." On March 15 he underwent surgery for lymphoma. The gristle—a malignant tumor—was removed along with lymph glands and pieces of the surrounding muscles.

Littler had played every Masters since he had turned pro in 1954. He handled the Augusta National course well. Indeed, he had only missed the cut twice in those eighteen tournaments. In 1970 he lost a championship play-off to Billy Casper. In 1971 he had finished fourth, just two shots behind the winner Charles Coody. He had every reason to believe he might win this time.

But as central as golf had been in his life, Littler actually found it easy to forgo the 1972 Masters—doctors said the surgery could be postponed for it—and let go of the tour life for a little while. "All I was interested in was survival," he would say later. In the months to come he would throw himself into the task, at one point even adopting a so-called zucchini diet that was supposed to keep the cancer at bay. The PGA Tour, and the glory of the Majors, would belong to someone else.

CHAPTER 3

*Augusta National happens to be the kind of course
that lends itself to the spectacular.*

−Grantland Rice

Augusta, Georgia, circa 1972 was the dowdy and worn-out home of 60,000 souls. The city rested on the banks of the muddy Savannah River, one hundred miles from the sea. In better days, Augusta had been a vibrant cotton center and winter resort. Then in 1916 a huge fire started by a tailor's unattended iron destroyed much of downtown. Five years later the boll weevil arrived to ruin cotton. Wealthy Northerners, who once brought a winter crop of cash, stopped coming as the railroads and developers seduced them to Florida. Over time, much of Augusta was overwhelmed by age and poverty.

For most of the year, in its quiet daily life Augusta was ordinarily little different from Macon or Greenville or any other small Southern city. Then came the first week of April.

On Monday cars from out of town began streaming in. By Wednesday night, Augusta's forty-odd hotels and motels were filled with visitors happy to pay $20 or $40 per night, twice the normal rates. By Thursday it would be impossible to find a bed at any price, even in one of the old boardinghouses. And restaurant reservations just couldn't be had. It was Masters week, and it seemed like everyone in the world wanted to be in Augusta, Georgia.

To be more precise, they wanted to be at Augusta National Golf Club. They found the place by driving down Washington Road, where the old brick houses squatted among flowering white dogwoods and azaleas. They passed under a huge banner that welcomed them to the club. Spectators searched for parking. Contestants looked for a sign marked Gate Two and turned down Magnolia Lane, which was flanked by sixty blossoming trees planted in the 1850s. The club's practice area lay to the left, behind the magnolias. To the right stretched a parking field big enough for 10,000 cars. Straight ahead, a little more than 300 yards distant, waited a two-story, white-columned mansion, as old as the magnolias.

Those who love the Masters and those who don't might agree on one thing. As you approach the graceful old clubhouse and leave Washington Road behind, Augusta National envelops you in a quiet, lush world apart. The golf course opened at the height of the Great Depression, in the same year—1932—that local author Erskine Caldwell's powerful novel *Tobacco Road* made the tragic lives of Augusta's poor sharecroppers known to the world. The National's stated purpose was to seclude its wealthy and privileged members from the tumult of the times. In this the club succeeded.

As Masters week arrived in 1972, there was much to escape. Monday brought news that the North Vietnamese Army had launched a massive armored attack on South Vietnam and its American allies. The North threw all but one of its divisions into what was called the Easter Offensive. By Thursday they would be within fifty miles of Saigon. America appeared to be on the verge of losing the war.

At home, businesses and workers were struggling with wage and price controls that President Nixon had imposed to stop inflation. The president had gone to Congress to seek help in ending court-ordered busing to integrate schools. And the Supreme Court, in a decision that opened the door to abortion rights, struck down a Massachusetts law denying contraception to single adults.

Americans who sought refuge from the trauma on the front page were confronted by more turmoil in the sports section. During Masters week, major league baseball players went on strike for the first time in history. The grand old game, once an inviolate symbol of wholesomeness, had fallen victim to the bitter resentments of players and the greed of owners. The players wanted substantially better pensions. The owners, angry about the erosion of their control over the athletes, stood fast against them.

Golf with its unchanging rules, and the Masters with its verdant pomp, offered a promising diversion. As the first Major of the year it signaled spring's arrival, the true beginning of the golf season, and the starting point for Jack Nicklaus's Grand Slam pursuit.

Everyone who played the Masters surely hoped he would win, but in the annual field of approximately eighty-five contestants, only a dozen or so could reasonably expect victory. Palmer, Player, and Nicklaus led the list. Beginning in 1960, one or another of these men had won the Masters seven years out of twelve. The three claimed second place six different times. And in one remarkable year—1965—all three finished atop the standings with Nicklaus first and the other two tied behind him.

Nicklaus believed he would leave the eighteenth green on Sunday with the title and the first milestone in his Grand Slam quest reached. He arrived at the tournament with more than $100,000 in PGA Tour winnings already banked. But he was not completely confident. A week of rain had deprived him of practice time. He felt edgy, a little less patient, and a little more introverted than usual. The hype surrounding the Grand Slam had invaded his mind and taken root. It added significantly to the pressure he typically applied to himself at every Major.

Nicklaus could take comfort in the fact that his booming drives gave him even more of an advantage at the National than they did at other courses. This is because his tee shots soared over many of its trickiest obstacles, especially slanted hillside lies that gave fits to less powerful hitters. Playing from more comfortable positions, he could attack the slippery greens with shorter, more lofted clubs (seven, eight, and nine irons), which made it easier for him to send the ball high and land it softly.

A young Jack Nicklaus had demonstrated this advantage very early in his career, during the 1964 Masters. His drive on the 520-yard fifteenth hole cleared a high mound that is roughly 250 yards from the tee, and just kept flying. The ball finally came to rest more than 350 yards from where it was struck. Nicklaus was almost as astonished as the gallery when he reached the ball, and he had trouble figuring out which club to use next. He chose an eight iron and watched in disappointment as it landed past the green. To get some idea of how remarkable this play was, consider that Ben Hogan, playing after Nicklaus, needed every bit of a four wood to reach the green on his second shot.

If Masters experience and the natural shape of Nicklaus's game made him the man most likely to win, these same factors conspired against Lee Trevino. For one thing, he played with a fade, which meant that his swing automatically sent his shots on a left-to-right path. Since most of the trouble at Augusta National lay on the right side of its fairways and greens, this was a problem. Then there was his troubled history with the tournament and its officials, which had caused him to decline previous invitations to play.

Though he had agreed to play this time, Trevino still avoided the clubhouse and locker room, holding to the excuse that it was simply more convenient to change shoes in the parking lot and go immediately to the practice range. He said the polite and proper things about being happy to be participating in the tournament. He repeatedly credited Nicklaus with persuading him to return, adding, "When Nicklaus tells an ant it can pull a bale of hay, you better hook him up right away." But for all of his good intentions, on his very first practice round Trevino got into a squabble that escalated into an argument that almost sent him home.

Trevino was playing with his regular tour caddie—Neal Harvey—walking along. On the eighth hole, one of the large contingent of police officers who handled security confronted Trevino and tried to throw Harvey off the course because he was wearing the wrong day's pass. Trevino was already annoyed that he had been forced to buy Harvey and his other guests their tickets—other tournaments simply gave them to contestants—so when the officer wouldn't show a little flexibility, he got angry.

"You ain't kicking him out," he said bluntly. "If he goes, I go."

With Trevino literally standing his ground on the fairway, and a crowd of onlookers growing, the policeman called for help. Tournament officials sent out the proper ticket, but Trevino still fumed. It was a ridiculous, disruptive incident, he thought, another example of high-handedness at the Masters. When he finished playing, he had a brief and unpleasant exchange of views with tournament chairman Roberts and then stalked off to his car. The reporters who trailed him heard him say something about leaving the tournament. In the end, he decided to stay and compete, but the fans and writers who were just waiting for him to explode took even more interest in his every move.

While Trevino was scrutinized like a bomb with a lighted fuse, most of the other competitors managed to practice in relative peace and quiet. One exception was Arnold Palmer, who was called to some extra celebrity duties. He posed for a cheek-to-cheek photo with Mamie Eisenhower and signed almost every scrap of paper thrust before him. He was good-natured, but he seemed weary as he yawned through some interviews. The graying of his hair was becoming more noticeable. He had begun to wear contact lenses to cope with presbyopia. But most of all, he was vexed by his play on the sixteenth hole at Greensboro the week before.

"Double bogey, triple bogey, bogey, and par," he almost chanted. "I had to hit a lot of bad shots to do that."

Most of Palmer's problems were in his putting. He was averaging about thirty-five putts per round, a good five or six too many if he intended to win. For many players the putting stroke is the first to fail as they age. It requires the most of the small muscles and reflexes that can grow stubborn with time.

Despite his difficulties, no one drew more supporters at the Masters than forty-two-year-old Palmer. His balky game and physical imperfections only made him more lovable to millions of fans. In 1972, the entire World War II generation was entering middle age. They, too, were dealing with the loss of youth, the challenge of stronger competitors, and the nagging suspicion that perhaps their best days were over. Among the thousands who came to follow him at the Masters, wearing buttons that read "I Love Arnie" and "I'm a member of Arnie's Army," were a great many who saw in him themselves.

Palmer drew people close with his personality, with the way he looked them in the eye and smiled as if he were seeing an old friend. Nicklaus awed them with his power and calm consistency in high-pressure championships. Golf fans in Augusta were keenly aware that with eleven Majors to his credit, Nicklaus was just two behind the record set by their beloved and recently departed Bobby Jones. Now that Nicklaus had declared his bid for the Slam, his string of Major victories was just about the only subject anyone wanted to hear him talk about. He chose to be as humble as he could without abandoning the goal. The Slam was possible, if not probable, he repeated. But for this week he was focusing on "this tournament right here," not the sweep.

On the same day that Trevino hassled with the police and Clifford Roberts, Nicklaus played a relaxed round and studied the greens. Augusta National's smooth bent-grass greens are occasionally afflicted with a fluffy invader called *poa annua* that affects the speed and direction of putts. This year the outbreak of the weed was especially severe, and as a result, many players were predicting high scores before the tournament began.

After his Tuesday workout on the course, Nicklaus sneaked off to the nearly deserted practice range to calibrate the artillery he would deploy in the first battle of the Grand Slam. Jackie Boy, as Jack Grout would have called him, was still worried about hitting enough shots. One after another, he sent balls arcing into the pale atmosphere, to the pines at the end of the range. The evening air grew chilly, darkness descended, and the scattering of onlookers thinned, but still he worked. Finally he teed up the last ball and applied just a little extra energy to it. It sailed over the trees, cleared the street beyond, and disappeared.

For eighteen years, the first Thursday in April had found Gene Littler on the number one tee of Augusta National Golf

Club making practice swings prior to the start of the Masters. In 1970 he had tied for first at the end of four days' play, only to lose an eighteen-hole play-off to Bill Casper.

But on the first day of the 1972 Masters, Gene Littler awoke in a bed at Mercy Hospital in San Diego. Orderlies arrived, transferred him to a gurney, and then wheeled him into an operating room. He was helped onto an operating table, where a mask was placed over his face. An anesthesiologist let gas flow, and he drifted into oblivion. Then the surgeon got to work, slicing through the skin, muscles, and nerves under his left arm. By the time he was through, Littler would lose more lymph nodes, more nerves, more muscle.

In the first hours after recovery, when survival was his only concern, Littler doubted he would play golf again. He could console himself with his record—twenty-four wins, a U.S. Open title, fifth in lifetime winnings. He had not prepared to let the game go. But in light of this catastrophe, cancer's invasion of his body, he believed his career was finished.

Three thousand miles to the east of San Diego, the warmth of a Georgia spring morning washed over Augusta National Golf Club, bathing it in a blossomed and scented glory. The temperature on this day would reach the mid-seventies, and the breeze was just enough to flutter the dogwood flowers. At 12:04 P.M. Jack Nicklaus stepped onto the first tee to strike his first shot in the first Major tournament of the year. The world was expecting a drive for the Slam. Nicklaus was worried about breaking 75 in both of the first two days and making the Friday cut, which would eliminate as much as half the field from the final two rounds. (Historically the dividing mark is a score of about 150.)

On the front nine, Nicklaus played like someone who *should* have been worried about making it to the weekend. He recovered from a bogey on the very first hole with a birdie on number two, a long par five that curves left to accommodate a power hitter's draw. But the putter just didn't feel right in Nicklaus's hands, and for the next nine holes he would struggle to get the ball into the cup. He made no birdies, and worse, one more bogey.

As Nicklaus reached the eleventh tee, the siren of a fire engine began to wail in the distance. It continued as he performed his preshot ritual right down to the little head tilt to the right that began his swing. A par four, the eleventh begins the series of three holes that golf writer Herbert Warren Wind named the Amen Corner back in 1958. Water comes into play on all three holes, and the wind can swirl in unpredictable ways. Number thirteen is dominated by a creek, which wanders down the left side of the fairway and then crosses it in front of the green. Together these holes can make any golfer pray.

With the fire siren howling, Nicklaus seemed to respond to the emergency in his round. On the eleventh green he rolled in a longish birdie putt—a twelve-footer—and felt for the first time that he had his putting under control. On number twelve, a short par three that is nevertheless the second toughest hole on the course, he reached the green with a seven iron and rolled in a twenty-five-footer for another birdie.

The two good putts brought Nicklaus to even par for the day and lifted him out of his funk. At 485 yards, hole number thirteen was one par five that even the weaker drivers could reach in two. Nicklaus put his second shot in a greenside bunker but got up and down for a birdie. He then followed a routine par with a performance on the fifteenth that was vintage Nicklaus.

Every hole at Augusta National is named for a tree or shrub that can be found on the course—Tea Olive, Pink Dogwood, Flowering Peach—and many ooze history. Number twelve and number thirteen are where Byron Nelson made up six whole strokes to beat Ralph Guldahl in 1937. Twenty years later, Doug Ford holed a shot from the bunker on eighteen to win his Green Jacket. Hole seventeen features the Eisenhower Pine, which guards the left side of the fairway roughly 200 yards from the tee. The president hit it so many times that he tried to have it cut down. The club refused to do it.

But none of Augusta's holes was more famous than the par-five fifteenth. This was where, in 1935, Gene Sarazen scored his famous double-eagle two (in those days it was also called an albatross) by holing a 230-yard four wood. Sarazen's feat established forever the Masters mystique. (Under Augusta National's favorite-son rules, former champions such as he had a permanent claim to a spot in the championship every year. Sarazen used his until 1974 when, at age seventy-two, he finally agreed he was no longer competitive. At the 1972 tournament, a pair of 79s left him on the wrong side of the cut. He hadn't been on the right side since 1963.)

When he played from the fifteenth tee on the first day of the Masters in 1972, Nicklaus drove to the right of the fairway, just one inch into the rough. He then faced the temptation that had been designed into the hole. Under good conditions most pros could hit the ball to the center of the green, about 240 yards away. This required carrying a pond just in front of it with a shot soft enough to stay put when it landed. A ball that flew too low and too fast might run through and into the water waiting beyond, along the adjacent fairway of the sixteenth hole. All day long players had thrilled the gallery by attempting the shot, but now a breeze was beginning to blow, complicating matters a bit.

Playing, as usual, without a hat, the blond-haired Nicklaus brought a large gallery down the fairway. Though Palmer remained the King of Augusta, the days when Nicklaus was the object of resentments and taunts were over. Now he was cheered by a gallery that appreciated his talents and his softer, more accessible personality. Younger fans, who had no prior allegiances, were especially loyal to him. On this day he wore fashionable clothes: white pants and a bronze and black shirt.

When Nicklaus reached his ball he made a thorough inspection and then chose a one iron—a club most pros found too difficult to hit well—for his second shot. He caught the ball perfectly, sending it into the headwind. It cleared the pond, landed in front of the hole, bounced, and then rolled about thirty feet. With his putting stroke in a groove, Nicklaus calmly rolled the ball in for an eagle.

Nicklaus shaved another stroke with an easy two on the sixteenth hole to finish the back nine a full five shots under par. Added to his first nine, he was four under for the day. That neat 68 put him just one stroke ahead of fifty-nine-year-old Sam Snead, who had played his first Masters three years before Nicklaus was born. Teeing off ahead of Nicklaus, Snead had three birdies on the first four holes. For the first time in a long time, he made a great many putts. He accomplished this with his famous "sidesaddle" stroke, which required him to set up facing the hole, with the ball to his right. With his hands set eighteen inches apart on the putter's shaft, he sort of pushed the ball toward its destination.

With his trademark coconut straw hat and slippery-smooth swing, Snead looked every bit the player he had been in the 1950s. He didn't make a bogey until the thirteenth, and even showed a little of his old power on the par fives. For a time, he was alone in first place on the scoreboard, the oldest man ever to hold that position at the Masters.

"I don't think I'd be here if I didn't use it," said Snead as he discussed the odd stroke that had allowed him to one-putt six greens. "I'm not embarrassed by having to putt this way, and I don't get as mad when I miss it." To keep the fellows in the pressroom amused, Snead threw some of his trademark country aphorisms into his remarks. One putt "swiveled up there like a peach seed." On a long drive he added a little "Cutty Sark" to make it fly. A ball caught in the breeze hovered "like one of those hawks about to dive."

While the press and gallery delighted in old Slammin' Sammy's performance, he could not reasonably expect to continue the pace. As the week wore on, the greens would get harder and faster and make more demands upon his shaky nerves. Even the balding Snead had to admit that the greens would have a lot of players "pulling their hair out." He was right. On the second day Snead's putting deteriorated and he scored a 75. This would be followed by a 76 and a 77. Although Snead had played one marvelous round, there was no fountain of youth out there in the Georgia pines.

On Thursday afternoon, Snead was followed closely by Arnold Palmer, all alone in third with a fine score of 70. With his eyes tearing from the heavy pollen in the air, Palmer had played the front of the course in two under par and the back in even par. He hit every fairway and his putting was remarkably solid.

For a while on Thursday, Gary Player matched Palmer, and the scoreboard read like it had in days gone by, with both of their names near the top with Snead's. But after going two under, Player gave back those strokes and more to finish with a 73. He was disappointed, but surely not as discouraged as Lee Trevino.

Still reluctant to use the locker room, Trevino had been met by a crowd as he changed shoes by his car in the parking lot. They trailed him to the practice range, to the putting green, to the first tee, and for his entire round. Many, no doubt, hoped to witness an eruption. Instead they saw a display of Trevino's newly enhanced ability to hit higher shots that could clear the troublesome hills in Augusta National's fairways and settle more softly on its hard greens. Unfortunately, they also saw him miss five putts of twelve feet or less and stumble to a double-bogey seven on the fabled fifteenth hole.

Trevino had believed he was playing the hole with intelligence. Refusing to be seduced by fifteen's reachable green, he laid up, in front of the pond. He would rather make a safe birdie or par than lose the gamble for an eagle. However, the fairway runs downhill to the pond and the green behind it, and he had to take a slightly awkward stance. He made a shaky swing and mishit his short iron. The ball plopped into the water. He kept his cool, though, never displaying his anger or frustration. After signing his scorecard for a round of 75 he managed to entertain the crowd in the parking lot.

"I didn't putt well," he confessed, "but I'll be back Friday, unless I have a heart attack."

Ironically, it was Nicklaus the leader who was a little up-tight in his postgame session with the press. "Here I am, worried about making the cut and breaking seventy-five," he said in his high, squeaky voice. "So it's pretty silly to be asked about the Grand Slam. I've still got some problems."

Nobody would have considered Paul Harney one of the obstacles Nicklaus would have to overcome at the Masters, not even Harney himself. Quiet and self-effacing, Harney was a capable player whose talents were known mainly by other pros and a few fans in his home state of Massachusetts. For nine years he had played only the first few months of each PGA Tour season, usually beginning in Los Angeles and finishing in Augusta, while his home course went from snow white to grassy green. Though he didn't play often enough to make a big name for himself, many older players recalled Harney's long drives and steady putting stroke. Nicklaus may have been the only player who could drive the ball farther than Harney with equal accuracy. Harney had been promising as a young pro. After two wins in 1957 he was invited to play a match with Billy Casper on the TV program *All Star Golf.* Harney also won the Los Angeles Open in 1964 and success-fully defended the title in 1965.

This year, Harney had found unexpected success on his

personal mini-tour. In Los Angeles he broke par every day and finished in the top twenty. He won the San Diego Open, his first victory in seven years, and was tenth at Doral. He arrived at Augusta ranked fourteenth on the money list with nearly $40,000 in winnings for the year, well ahead of many better-known players.

On Friday at the Masters, Harney began play three strokes behind the leader. He had been one of just five players to break par the day before, but the performances of Nicklaus, Snead, and Palmer—and the mere appearance of Lee Trevino—had obscured this feat. Just a handful of people followed Harney and his playing partner, noted amateur Jim Simons, after they left the first tee a few minutes after noon.

As he moved down the fairway and put the clubhouse behind him, Paul Harney knew he was one of just a few players who were truly comfortable at Augusta National. He had played the tournament eight times before, always making the cut, and always making a good paycheck. He had four top tens, including a fifth-place finish in 1964, the year Palmer won by six strokes. And he was not intimidated by the field.

"It is the weakest in any Major," recalled Harney, years later. "I mean, they invite a lot of foreign champions who don't play the American tour and are really not prepared. Then there are all the past champions. A lot of them aren't going to make the cut. By the time you take away the people who don't hit the ball in a way that suits the course, you're really only competing against about twenty guys."

Hitting the ball with smooth authority, Harney seemed to knock every iron shot to within ten feet of the flagstick on every green. He made a solid putt on number twelve for a birdie two. Then, in a beautiful display of his strength, he used an easy three wood and a four iron to score an eagle on thirteen. Of course, scoring requires good putting, and Harney had this, too. He needed only twenty-nine putts in a round of 69.

As he walked to the clubhouse, the leaderboard showed that Nicklaus, playing behind Harney, was two under for the day and poised to run away with the tournament. But by the time Harney reached the pressroom for his postround interview, a double-bogey seven—caused by a second shot that found the water—had been posted by Nicklaus on the fifteenth hole. Though Nicklaus would birdie the last hole to get back into first place alone, Harney was for a moment tied for the lead after two days at the Masters.

Suddenly confronted with the fact that he was now a true contender, Paul Harney was embarrassed by the attention he received. When pressed to assess his chances he finally choked out an answer: "I don't know if I can win it, but maybe I can if I keep this up."

In contrast, Nicklaus seemed much more comfortable than he had been on Thursday. He joked that together, the seven and the eagle three he had carded in two days on the fifteenth hole averaged out to par. And he said he was eager to play the weekend rounds and settle the championship. He even seemed more patient with Grand Slam questions, allowing that he enjoyed the attention, even though it meant added pressure.

It was likely that Nicklaus's comfort level came from the scores he could see being marked next to the names of the opponents he feared the most. Four-time Masters champion

Arnold Palmer, of the watery eyes and aching hip, couldn't maintain the play that had earned him a 70 the day before. His real troubles began on the ninth hole, then got worse.

On the ninth, Palmer's second shot skidded off the green and came to rest in a little hole made by the leg of an on-looker's folding metal chair. Since the turf had been altered by the hand—or in this case chair leg—of man, Palmer considered this "ground under repair" and wanted a free drop. A rules official said no. Fuming, Palmer putted the original ball and missed by ten feet. After making bogey, he dropped a second ball and made par. He then lodged an appeal with the full rules committee.

There was good reason for Palmer to take this step. Fourteen years earlier, at the 1958 Masters, he had followed one of his tee shots to discover his ball similarly embedded. That time he had also played the original to a bogey and returned to play a second ball for par. Rules officials eventually decided that the embedded ball rule applied. The soft terrain had captured the first shot and accordingly he was entitled to the drop. Remarkably, Palmer went on to win that Masters by the margin of the two shots he had gained with that ruling.

This time the ruling went against Palmer. The committee relayed its decision as he walked off the eleventh green. The bogey would stand.

On the next tee Palmer refused to say how he felt, but his face showed the anger boiling inside. (This is why people liked him. He showed his feelings.) He promptly hit an eight iron into the bunker that fronted the green. With his blood pressure and adrenaline level rising, he blasted out and over the green to the rough on the back side. A weak chip and three putts later and he had a total of six on a par-three hole. Banished earlier in the week, the memory of a similar triple bogey and the tournament loss in Greensboro came back to him. A final score of 75 reflected perfectly the state of his mind.

With the cut set at 151 strokes—high by Masters standards—Palmer made it easily. Somehow Lee Trevino managed to play even worse than he had on Thursday. But his score of 76 placed him right on the cutline, qualifying him for weekend play. He was so far out of contention, though, that the leaders could ignore him. He declined a request that he appear in the pressroom, arguing that his performance had been so poor that he didn't deserve the attention. Tracked down at his car/dressing room, he bristled when the subject turned to next year's Masters. "Don't ask me that question," he said. "I'm already in enough trouble."

Paul Harney spent a sleepless night in Augusta before Saturday's tee-off. It wasn't that he was afraid; he was just excited, and so keyed up by the prospect of a championship run that his mind wouldn't settle down. Of course, the worry about how little sleep he was getting only made things worse. When the sun finally came up, he had barely rested. Weekend tee times were set so that the leaders would go out last and the afternoon TV coverage would have something good to show. This meant Harney had to wait around until two o'clock in the afternoon, by which time he was completely exhausted.

Harney was paired on Saturday with a journeyman pro from Illinois who was truly shocked to find himself in contention. Dressed in plaid pants and a stretched-out cardigan, 220-

pound Jim Jamieson looked just like the fellows you can find in the taproom of every clubhouse in America. Born in 1944, he had taken up the game at the age of nine. He had inked the names of his heroes—Hogan, Snead, Palmer—onto golf balls and then played fantasy tournaments against himself at a nine-hole course in Moline. By age ten he broke 40. In 1969, with the founder of the Dairy Queen chain of ice cream stands as his backer, Jamieson became a touring pro.

In two days at Augusta, Jamieson had managed to play some of his best golf against a challenging course, scoring first a steady 72 and then a two-under-par 70. He did this with a collection of golf clubs that resembled the lost-and-found barrel at a driving range. He used Golfcraft woods, a mix of irons from Ping and Spalding, and wedges made by Powerbilt, Hagen, and Hogan. A few weeks earlier, he had walked into Iveys Department Store in Orlando and spied a putter in the sporting goods section. It was labeled "Tour Pro Model" and had a leather grip that felt good in Jamieson's hand. He bought the club for $17.50, but passed on some golf balls that the salesman had assured him rather breathlessly, "are the same ones used by Arnold Palmer!"

The department-store putter was put to good use at the Masters, where Jamieson's excellent short game helped him attack the pins. This was especially helpful at Augusta, where holes were typically located so near to obstacles like bunkers and water that getting close required precision. "I hit it pretty straight, kept it in play, so I was always able to play well on hard golf courses," he would recall years later. "Sixty percent of the game is from one hundred yards in. That's where I really played well."

Though he felt confident in his basic abilities, at Augusta, Jamieson was as nervous as a boy at his first Little League tryout. He felt it in his stomach, in his knees, and in his hands. On Saturday morning he was so distracted that he forgot to bring tees. On the practice range he shyly asked Nicklaus to give him a few. At first Nicklaus casually tossed him a couple. Then he grabbed a handful, walked over to Jamieson, and put them in his golf bag.

"They got your name on them?" teased Jamieson.

"That's the only kind I got," came the reply.

"Okay if I throw them in the rough?"

Rather than disturb his game, Jamieson's jittery feelings somehow helped him to focus more intently. "I've never concentrated like I have this week," he commented. "Every shot. It's amazing."

Jamieson delighted in his role as a surprise actor in the Masters drama. A puckish character with a huge grin and impossibly sunny attitude, the gallery loved him. On a chilly, blustery Saturday he attracted a large following, not as large as the one that walked with Nicklaus, but enough to raise a ruckus when Jamieson played well.

There was much to cheer on the back nine. While Harney played his worst round so far and would finish with a 75, Jamieson made a Palmer-style charge. On the fourteenth hole, he struck a six iron that sent the ball to five feet from the hole, and then he made the birdie putt. He made a much longer putt—twenty feet—to steal another stroke from par on the fifteenth. Feeling more excited than he may have ever felt on a golf course, Jamieson nailed a nine-iron shot to eight feet from the hole and got his third birdie in a row on seventeen.

On Saturday afternoon Jamieson received the loudest ovation of his career as he marched down the eighteenth fairway. Virtually unknown, and entirely unglamorous, he had won the support of thousands. He missed the green and then failed to make his par putt. But he nevertheless recorded one of the best scores of the day—70—and wound up just one shot behind Nicklaus. Harney was two shots back of Jamieson, tied for third place with young Tom Weiskopf.

A 70 had brought Weiskopf to a three-day score of 215, one under par. At almost any other tournament, on any other golf course, this wouldn't be nearly good enough to get a man close to first place. But at Augusta, where shots that were merely good wouldn't suffice, and the greens required the steady hands of a neurosurgeon, three rounds played to a total of one under par put Weiskopf in contention. This wasn't quite good enough for the tempestuous Weiskopf, however. He considered the last nine holes he had played the best golf of his life and was so disappointed with his score he could be heard muttering a string of curse words as he left the eighteenth green.

Of course, none of the runners-up would have found themselves so close to the top if Jack Nicklaus had not committed a string of uncharacteristic errors and squandered much of the five-stroke lead he had built up early in the day. Nicklaus had played so well through the twelfth hole that he had begun to think that he might add another two or three strokes to his lead before the day was done. After all, the third of the course he had yet to play included some of his best opportunities for birdies.

But as Nicklaus tried to cope with the wind, something went wrong with his well-tooled swing. He began to hook the ball to the left. This problem put him into a bunker on the thirteenth and almost landed him in trouble on fourteen. On the treacherous fifteenth, site of his Friday double bogey, he overshot the green again and had to settle for a par on a hole where he always hoped for an eagle.

It was difficult to understand why Nicklaus would knock his ball over the fifteenth hole for a second day in a row, even if the wind made club selection tricky. But what he did on the seventeenth defied explanation. Still fighting the hook, he pulled his nine-iron approach shot, leaving the ball just off the green. There his eyes fooled him as he lined up to strike the ball. He was certain the cup was uphill from where he stood, and that he had to apply a little extra power to reach it. But as the crowd that circled the green could plainly see, the hole was actually downhill. Nicklaus rapped the ball firmly. It rolled past the cup and then kept on going until it was off the green again on the opposite side. It took two more tries for Nicklaus to hole it.

Ironically, even as Nicklaus was stumbling around the back nine, Lee Trevino stood before the press praising him as a superstar who could beat God himself "on a wide open course." After recording his worst score yet, a 77, Trevino had finally given in to the requests for him to visit the press-room. (This may have had something to do with the cold wind that swept the parking lot where he had done all his talking so far.) He explained his own performance with the candid admission that he had a "mental block" that prevented him from playing well at Augusta. "I'll probably shoot eighty tomorrow," he lamented. Then he turned to one of his favorite subjects, Nicklaus.

Sitting in a green leather chair set on a small stage, Trevino chewed on a stick of gum and grinned as he offered his analysis. "I said two years ago he's the best the game has ever seen. He's a freak," he laughed. "He's so strong he plays a different golf course. In fact, he might even beat two people. He can beat our best ball."

Out on the course, Nicklaus was not playing at all like someone who could handle a match that was two-against-one. Coming up the eighteenth fairway behind Jamieson, Nicklaus found his drive and then began to worry about his swing mechanics. After a long wait, he finally hit a low, hooked five iron toward the green. The ball found a greenside bunker where it would be no easy up and down for par. Instead another bogey, suffered as the afternoon shadows grew long, dropped his lead to one slim stroke. This was no way to win the Masters, let alone begin the Grand Slam.

The five iron into eighteen had been the product of one of the worst swings Nicklaus had made in months, if not years. But rather than panic, he saw this event as an oddity that could be quickly corrected. After the round he went to the driving range and in twenty minutes seemed to have it solved. (He mentioned something technical about the movement of his legs.) He then asked a TV crew to turn its lights on the practice green. With his caddie standing by, Nicklaus rolled sixteen little putts from a distance of ten feet. He made about half of them, including the last three in a row. When he looked up after the last putt, he had a smile on his face. "I don't know if that was work or superstition," he confessed. Whatever it was, it made him feel better.

Without a Palmer, Trevino, or Player in sight, Jack Nicklaus held every advantage at the start of the final round. His closest pursuer, the roly-poly Jamieson, had never won a regular tour event, let alone a Major. As he arrived at the course Jamieson kept saying he was just happy to be there. "Whatever I shoot, I'm a winner," he told a reporter. "And I'm nervous. Put that down." It was hardly the talk of a serious contender.

Harney and Weiskopf were more formidable competitors. Weiskopf had bested Nicklaus early in the year at Fort Lauderdale. Harney had won early in the year at San Diego and was too experienced to be intimidated. But he was not immune to illness. As it would turn out, a virus had overtaken him in the night. Harney would be followed all day by a doctor, who checked him as he grew weaker and weaker.

So it was left to the hotheaded Weiskopf and the startled young Jamieson to somehow prevent Nicklaus from reaching the first of his four Grand Slam goals. Jamieson was hoping to be lucky. On Saturday night, he and the crowd of people who were sharing a house near the course reenacted events of the night before, right down to the chicken dinner they ate and the seating arrangement at the table. On Sunday he went to a distant corner of the practice range to prepare and tried to stay out of the limelight.

Jamieson was paired with the ailing Harney in the next-to-last group. They teed off at 1:16 P.M., eight minutes ahead of Nicklaus and Weiskopf. It would be one of the strangest final rounds in Masters history, a sort of sleepwalk as almost everyone played defensively against a course with wickedly fast greens and pin placements that were impossible to attack.

Trembling and just a little disbelieving, Jamieson bogied the first, third, and fifth holes. As any pro will tell you, pressure takes its toll first on the short game, and Jamieson's early troubles were with putting and chipping. But just about everything that could go wrong, did. On number twelve, a seemingly easy 155-yard par three, he cleared a creek, but his heart sank as the ball hit the slope leading up to the green, bounced, and then rolled backward into the drink. At that moment he forgot about chasing the leader and began worrying about breaking 80, the threshold many pros set for what constitutes a truly embarrassing round.

He would avoid humiliation by finishing with a 77. (Harney suffered to a virally induced 81.) When it was over, Jamieson would confess that Augusta National, under such conditions, was just too tough for him. He had company. Only a handful of players would come in under par 72. Not a single one would score lower than 70.

Playing behind Jamieson, the Golden Bear—dressed this day in a golden-colored sweater—carefully picked his way along the course as each of his three pursuers bogeyed the first hole, and then two more, before reaching number five. They literally handed the tournament to Nicklaus, who finished the front nine in one under par. Six strokes ahead, with just nine holes to play, Nicklaus still had to contend with greens as hard and fast as stainless steel. On the eleventh hole he made a three-putt bogey. From that point on he would play safe, aiming for greens, not flagsticks, for pars, not bogeys.

Weiskopf struggled to challenge Nicklaus. But he was punished for every risk he took, and under the tough conditions could not muster a run of birdies. The frustration Weiskopf felt was plain on his face. No one revered the Masters more than Weiskopf. When it was over, and he had failed, he sounded much like Walter Hagen airing his frustrations over Bobby Jones and his fellow pros at the U.S. Open in 1926. "With nobody pressuring him," complained Weiskopf, "he [Nicklaus] played great golf."

"Great" was an exaggeration. From the tenth tee inward, Nicklaus played like someone trying not to lose. He almost failed. On the thirteenth hole he three-putted from fifty feet. Then on fourteen he faced a long putt from the fringe. He hit it past the hole and off the green on the opposite side. Two more putts gave him a bogey. On the very next hole, fifteen, Nicklaus played as cautiously as he could, mindful of the fact that he had placed his second shot over the green twice already in the tournament. He chose to hit a four iron and still hit through the green. This time, though, the ball stopped just short of the water. He missed the green entirely with a sculled chip shot, then he couldn't make a three-footer for par. In retrospect, he was probably lucky to walk away with a simple bogey.

Coming in to the seventeenth hole, Nicklaus's lead was down to two strokes. Weiskopf was now playing steadily, and it was conceivable that Nicklaus could give the whole thing away. On his second shot, an eight iron, Nicklaus put his ball in the bunker, where it burrowed halfway into the sand. He somehow managed to get it out but needed to make a tricky right-to-left putt from eleven feet. At last he was able to read the break and the speed perfectly. He got his par.

On another golf course, in another tournament, such an ugly performance by Sunday's leader would have likely been matched by an aggressive string of birdies from a challenger. But this was the Masters, played on a golf course that can snarl like a dragon and make any player quake. Add the *poa annua* infestation of the greens, and you have a pretty good explanation for all the high scores.

Despite shooting a 74, his worst round of the week, Nicklaus walked up the eighteenth fairway with the title in hand. With the gallery cheering, Weiskopf put his arm around Nicklaus's shoulders and said, "I wish I could have given you a better fight."

Who knows what a better fight would have brought out in Nicklaus's game that day? Weiskopf himself would later say that the Bear would have risen to any challenge, abandoned his safe strategy, and won anyway. But the truth was, his winning score was seven shots higher than Charles Coody's a year before. And in thirty-six years only three winning scores had been higher. One of those was posted by Nicklaus himself in 1966.

It could have been the greens, or the pressure, but no matter the cause, no one was better than Nicklaus at the 1972 Masters, where 286 was three shots lower than the next best score. Nicklaus joined Palmer as the only four-time winners of the Masters, drew within one of the Bobby Jones lifetime record for Major wins, and completed the first of the four laps he would need to win the Slam. He did all this while coping with the enormous pressure of his self-made competition with the deceased Jones. Nicklaus had devised this contest with a ghost, made it public, and then lived up to its challenge.

With his success, Nicklaus finally relaxed enough to admit that he had begun the year thinking he could well win all four, and now his chances were much improved. The next challenge would be the U.S. Open at Pebble Beach. In the two months leading up to it, "I'll be thinking about Pebble Beach, about playing the types of shots I'll need to win there."

Among Nicklaus's chief competitors, only Gary Player would leave Augusta with a completely clear mind and heart. Though he had been disappointed by Lee Elder's absence, Player avoided controversy at Augusta and managed to play steady golf, saving his best—a one-under-par 71—for the last day. On Sunday he had quietly crept into tenth place. He then quickly left Augusta to compete with Elder in the United Golf Association tournament.

Lee Trevino's final eighteen holes were played in an even-par 72 strokes, his best of the week. Afterward, he stayed around Augusta National long enough to accept Clifford Roberts's invitation for a little stroll around the very same clubhouse he had self-consciously avoided. They spent time in the trophy room and gazed at a display of Bobby Jones's sand wedge. Noting the nicks in the blade, Trevino had said, "I guess he played in a lot of rocks."

The overture made by the tournament chairman was a significant gesture, given that Trevino had declined Roberts's invitation to coffee earlier in the week with a sarcastic reply: "Just tell Mr. Roberts I don't drink coffee." Trevino had instantly regretted what he had said, and was relieved to have a chance to make up for it. Afterward he spoke as if he had finally heard the call and was ready to testify to the glory of the Masters. He would return, he said, whenever invited.

As a past champion, Arnold Palmer could rightfully return to Augusta every spring for as long as he wanted. But the way he played Sunday may have given him second thoughts about ever coming back at all. He confessed to giving up on the fourth hole. Considered one of the toughest on the course, this par three requires a 200-yard tee shot, which most players make with a long iron. Palmer hit what appeared to be a perfect shot but just caught the top of a bunker and found himself in the sand. He hit his bunker shot out and over the green and eventually made a double bogey. Later in the round the head flew off his seven iron during his swing. An appropriate metaphor, perhaps, for the overall state of his game.

"I have never played before a more quiet gallery," recalled his playing partner Bruce Devlin. "He did not go down fighting."

Palmer was embarrassed by his score of 81, the worst he had ever posted in eighteen years at the Masters. No one who had played all four days of the tournament shot a higher score. If this performance didn't have Palmer thinking about whether his championship days were over, it certainly occurred to many other pros. He just wasn't the player he had been. Indeed, he wasn't even keeping up with others his age, such as Harney and Bob Rosburg, who had both won tournaments that season.

The sight of the embattled old king of golf walking up the eighteenth fairway moved the thousands who stood behind the ropes to take to their feet and cheer. He climbed onto the green and raised his right arm to acknowledge the welcome. Later in the day, Jack Nicklaus would feel the gallery's appreciation. At this moment, Palmer received its love. He had earned it, many years before, and nothing he could do on the golf course would diminish it. After he finished play, Palmer would be mobbed by fans. He signed countless autographs and even allowed one overwhelmed female admirer to kiss his hand.

"The people at Augusta just loved him," recalled Col. Joe Curtis, a close friend of Palmer's who had witnessed his every shot at the Masters. "It wasn't about his winning. It was about the way he looked at people, how they felt they knew exactly what he was feeling. It's something we talked about a lot, but couldn't explain. A lot of people just felt connected to him."

On the day after the Masters, an eleven-year-old boy stood by the fence that guarded the runway at Augusta's little airport. Like many young boys, Victor DellaGiustina loved airplanes, and he often walked to the airstrip to watch them take off. On this morning, he was feeling the letdown that always follows the conclusion of the Masters.

Victor had spent his weekend wearing a big Arnie's Army button and trooping from hole to hole with the big family that was Palmer's legion in Augusta. A year earlier, he had been introduced to the King by a neighbor, who had hosted a big party for Palmer. Victor had been invited in recognition of his tenth birthday. He had stared, wide-eyed, at the smiling man's huge arms and felt the power as Palmer had taken his small hand in his own. From that moment, Victor's loyalty was sealed. And for the next thirty years he would witness every round that his hero played at Augusta National.

Standing by the fence on that warm April morning, Victor truly believed that his hero would win the Masters again one day. He watched several small prop planes skitter down the pavement and into the air until, at last, came the Learjet marked with the registration number 701AP. Its engines whined at a higher and higher pitch as it rapidly accelerated down the runway and became airborne. Victor kept his eye on it until it became a speck in the sky, and then disappeared. Later that day, at St. Mary's School, he would argue with his friends that despite the outcome at the Masters, Arnold Palmer was the best golfer alive. While most of the boys held fast in their commitment to the younger, harder-hitting Nicklaus, Victor would later recall that he had persuaded a few.

Learjet 701AP headed north, to Palmer's hometown of La-trobe, Pennsylvania. Forty miles from Pittsburgh, Latrobe was a place of foundries and three-decker houses and neighbor-hood taverns. Palmer would sometimes pop into one of these places, where he would meet men who spent their days in hard physical labor, and be reminded of the good fortune he enjoyed, even on his worst day of tournament play.

Latrobe was where Palmer found both refuge and reju-venation. It was also where he would find two of his most trusted advisers, his mother and father. His mother, Doris, offered unconditional love. His father, Milfred "Deacon" Pal-mer, called him back to the smalltown values of his youth. As superintendent and then the pro at the Latrobe Country Club, Deacon had taught Arnold the basics of golf and life. Arnold got to play on the course only when members were not around. He never once swam in the club's pool. He earned nickels fetching balls out of the ditch that ran across the club's sixth fairway. Later he'd get fifty cents per round as a caddie.

Coming home to Latrobe always reminded Arnold Palmer of the value of hard work and the blessings he had received through golf. After a few days there, his scores at the Masters became less troubling, and his optimism about the rest of the Tour '72 schedule began to return.

CHAPTER 4

Of all the people I have met in sports—or out—
Jones came the closest to what we call a great man.
—Herbert Warren Wind

At 3 P.M. on May 4, 1972, the members of the Town Council of St. Andrews, Scotland, donned crimson robes and ermine stoles and joined a procession that wound through the old village to Holy Trinity Church. In the churchyard, a signboard announced "A Memorial and Thanksgiving." The oak doors of the fifteenth-century stone building were opened and more than one hundred souls filed in.

Pain and loss were plain on the faces of those who had come on a chilled afternoon to honor Bobby Jones. His son and daughter-in-law sat in the first pew, bathed in the soft light filtered by the blue and brown stained glass. Upon the altar was placed a silver golf club adorned with silver golf balls, one for each man who had served as captain of the Royal and Ancient Golf Club since 1754. Eleven living captains accompanied the ceremonial club to the church to honor a man who, in the minister's words, "gave light and encouragement to all whose lives he touched."

The affection that Scots in general, and citizens of St. Andrews in particular, felt for Bobby Jones was long-standing. When Jones made his first visit in 1921, they were the ones who had named him "Bobby." (Previously he had been called Robert T. Jones, Jr., and nothing else.) The bond was made permanent at the 1930 British Amateur Championship, where the American's personal style and peerless golf dazzled the galleries.

The tournament was played on the Old Course at St. Andrews. Jones dominated a long series of matches, defeating both British and American contenders. In the finals he met Roger Wethered before a crowd of 15,000. He was seven holes ahead, with six to play, when the thirty-six-hole contest ended. He needed a police escort to escape the adoring gallery.

From that day on, every round that Jones ever played at St. Andrews, even his unannounced, casual outings, attracted huge crowds. Word would spread that "our Bobby" was on the course, and hundreds would go out to watch him play. In 1958, he was made a citizen of St. Andrews, the first American to be so honored since Benjamin Franklin was granted the privilege 201 years prior. Nearly 2,000 people attended the ceremony.

The gathering that honored Jones in death was held after the annual meeting of the St. Andrews Club. The principal speaker was the same Roger Wethered who had been overwhelmed by Jones at the Amateur in 1930. A beefy old man dressed in a black suit and black tie, Wethered rose unsteadily to the lectern and peered through thick glasses at the notes he had made. He then spoke of Jones's "artistry, simplicity, modesty, and straightforward look. His presence alone," added Wethered, "gave you a wonderfully good feel.

"I count myself unbelievably fortunate to have played with Bobby at the height of his majestic powers," continued Wethered. Then he offered what may have been the ultimate praise that a Scot of his time might give to a golfing man. "He was," said Wethered, "the complete master of himself."

Whatever one might make of Bobby Jones's complex character, in golf he was the master of himself. This he had demonstrated time and again during close competition. While he felt sickeningly nervous in Major tournaments, the turmoil inside never showed, and he was able to play with an unmatched level of concentration. Jones was also fully in command of his golfing career. He played golf as a game, valued his amateur status, and always resisted the lure of the significant wealth he could have had playing as a professional.

Except for Nicklaus's pursuit of the Majors, Jones would have had only mild interest in the golf season of 1972. Ordinary pro tournaments held no appeal for him in his long life as a spectator. This attitude—a matter of taste, really—had served his image as a golfing purist, and it had made the Calvinists among golf fanatics love him even more.

Like Jones, Nicklaus cherished the Majors. He also burned to match and then succeed Jones as the best player in the game's history. This could only be done at the big four tournaments of the year. At the start of the 1972 season he had explained this to a *Los Angeles Times* writer: "I would like to accomplish things so that, when you look back, you can say I was better. As far as I am concerned, the best way to compare golfers is the number of Major tournaments they have won."

Unlike Jones, who was a lawyer and industrialist, Nicklaus had no business interests outside the game that would support his family. He needed to play the pro circuit. His victories earned him prize money but also built a public image that was worth more. The annual race to be first on the money list at the end of the tour was also important to him, not so much because he wanted the cash, but because he was a compulsive competitor. If it was possible to keep score, no matter the activity, he wanted to win.

Anyone who doubts that Nicklaus prized the tour's annual money title can refer to a telling passage in Arnold Palmer's 1999 autobiography, *A Golfer's Life*. In it, Palmer describes the heated battle he had with Nicklaus over the 1964 money crown. As the last tournament of the year arrived, Palmer led by about $300. Both men said they doubted they would go to Lafayette, Louisiana, for the Cajun Classic. The tournament was beneath consideration, they agreed, a low-rent, backwater event best left to the stragglers hoping to keep their playing status. Then they both signed up.

Through wind and rain and then near-freezing temperatures, Palmer and Nicklaus battled to see who would make more money at the Cajun Classic and finish on top for the year. Nicklaus prevailed, finishing second and grabbing enough cash to leap ahead of Palmer, who came in fourth. It was, he said, the first time in his life he was happy about being runner-up in a tournament.

Under normal circumstances Nicklaus avoided the Cajun Classic and all the other low-status events on the PGA Tour. His strategy for piling up his annual winnings was based on victories where the purses were richest. Three or four first-place finishes—at $30,000 apiece—could get a player halfway to the top of the heap. For anyone else, assuming even one victory a year was bold. But Nicklaus's average number of wins per year was 3.75. Combine this with fifteen top-ten finishes, and it's easy to see how he could dominate the money list while playing as few as eighteen tournaments.

In 1972, with the Masters and two other wins already pocketed, Nicklaus didn't even have to think about attending the next tour stop, in Pensacola. He would skip it and then compete the following week in the Tournament of Champions in La Costa, California. Only the previous year's winners were invited, and Nicklaus enjoyed the challenge of facing the best of his competitors.

At the start of the Tournament of Champions, one of the players who received the most attention had been forced to withdraw from the competition. Conversations in the locker room came to a stop as Gene Littler, looking thin and pale, came through the door. La Costa wasn't far from his home, and Littler had come to bask in the ambiance of the event. Though he was shy about discussing the details, he had already begun rehabilitation, trying to train the left side of his body to compensate for lost muscle. For the moment, he couldn't even make half a backswing.

On the positive side, and this Littler told everyone, his surgery had been a complete success. All the cancer was gone from his body. His doctors had told him he could pick up a club in a month and start to swing it in two. What happened after that would be a matter of physiology and determination. If he could train the muscle that remained to compensate for the flesh that had been taken, he would play again.

"Privately, I was very worried," said Littler, long after he had healed. "My arm was swollen to twice its normal size and I was missing pectoral muscle, latissimus, trapezius."

Littler was worried because pro golf was how he supported his family. At La Costa he said all the right things about being glad to be alive and hoping for a comeback. But he didn't fully believe it himself.

Once the tournament began, Littler went home and all eyes turned to Jack Nicklaus. Everywhere he played, Nicklaus was considered "the man to beat," and if anyone outside the ranks of the superstars happened to beat him, it was cause for the celebration of an underdog. Many of Nicklaus's fine performances were overlooked because someone else happened to have one of the best weeks of his life and finished a stroke ahead of the favorite.

This is just what happened at La Costa, two weeks after the 1972 Masters. Bobby Mitchell scored a birdie on the first play-off hole to beat Nicklaus. In six years on tour, Mitchell had won just once, at the 1971 Cleveland Open. He was best known for the toupee he had begun to wear six months earlier, and for the fact that he had quit school in the tenth grade to become an assistant pro at a Virginia golf course. His win at La Costa would be the second and last PGA Tour victory of his entire life. But in managing to beat Nicklaus head-to-head, he obscured the fact that Nicklaus had followed up his Masters win by finishing tied for first against a much tougher field at the very next event he played.

Nicklaus was unfazed as the press fawned over Mitchell, calling him a "giant killer" and "the invisible man." He had his own priorities—the upcoming U.S. Open being first—and his own way of preparing. He would skip five of the next seven tournaments, choosing to rest and practice rather than scramble for dollars. The way he saw it, there was little to be gained from sweating it out in Houston or Memphis or Philadelphia, and much benefit to be had from a deliberate practice routine and daily life with his wife, Barbara, and their then four children.

In the month before the Open, Nicklaus played in just a single event, the Atlanta Classic. On the Tuesday before the tournament he flew in on his private plane for a quick practice round. He said he wanted to win, naturally, but his main purpose was to tune up for the Open. He wanted to test his legs after three weeks away from walking a course. He played well in practice, and on the tournament's second day shot a course-record 64. This was matched by a final-round 76, his worst score of the year. He never came close to winning, but no one took this to mean anything about how he would perform in the Open. Nicklaus performed his best only when the stakes were high enough—when he cared enough—to be nervous. The Atlanta Classic did not make him nervous.

Lee Trevino had approached the tour year with the same goals as Nicklaus—Major victories, tournament wins, a big earnings total—but in a different order. He focused much more intently on the dollars. He was driven, first, by a poor boy's hunger. Having never had money, he now enjoyed it, almost too much. He was determined to secure real wealth for his children, and he needed cash flow for his growing business interests, which were fed in part from his earnings from tournaments. For this reason, he played as often as he could.

With the unfamiliar demands of outside business—filming commercials, appearing at sponsors' events, negotiating contracts—Trevino was hard-pressed to find time for his practice routine. He had no Jack Grout to provide quick answers to his swing problems. Instead, his habit was to hit hundreds of practice balls and play as many rounds as possible. This was how he found a groove for his swing and kept it.

Trevino held to a very firm set of beliefs about the importance of playing and practicing. On a superstitious level, he feared that fate, or God, would be on his side only if he worked hard. The dedication and sweat made him deserving. But on a more practical note, he knew that hitting hundreds and hundreds of balls per day raised his confidence.

"My subconscious knew," he would one day explain, "if I had paid the price to win. If I had worked hard there was no way I would choke. If I hadn't, and I knew it deep down, I might."

True to his hard-work ethic, Trevino took the opposite approach to Nicklaus's tour scheduling. Coming out of the Masters, Trevino had earned less than $45,000 in the year, much less than Nicklaus, who had already passed $135,000. Determined to catch up, Trevino decided to play as many events as possible. He believed he was setting the odds in his favor, like the salesman who will ring a hundred doorbells every day.

"If I got five hundred dollars or fifty thousand dollars, that was all money I wouldn't have gotten if I stayed home," he explained after retiring from the regular PGA Tour. "The fact that I was making it playing golf was even better."

The trouble was, tournament golf at its highest levels isn't just a matter of persistence. And it doesn't always reward extra toil. Winning golf depends as much on the mind as it does the body, and rest is vital for both.

After the Masters, Jack Nicklaus took nearly two weeks away from competition to prepare for the Tournament of Champions in California. Palmer also took time away from the tour, while Gary Player went all the way home to South Africa. (He would win the Japan Airlines Open while abroad and return to play at Pebble Beach.) But Lee Trevino went to Pensacola, Florida, where a $30,000 first prize and a field devoid of any of the other top players beckoned at the Monsanto Open.

The result was disastrous. On the first day Trevino's feet felt leaden and his mind was almost as heavy. He couldn't break par on the short and easy Pensacola Country Club Course. He then trundled into the pressroom, slumped in a chair, and announced his withdrawal.

"It's been coming on for some time," he said. "Then last week at the Masters I was under tremendous pressure. I came here just drained. I'm absolutely exhausted and I just want to go home and rest up for the Tournament of Champions."

It was bad news for the tournament, its sponsors, and fans in Pensacola, all of whom depended on Trevino to give the tournament some energy. It was worse for Trevino himself, who felt too exhausted to follow through on his commitment and ended up deprived of the rest he would have banked if he had gone home in the first place. Worst of all, he was beginning to doubt himself, to worry that he might never win again.

Weary as he may have been, Trevino was a strong man, the kind who could drink heavily, stay up all night, and somehow manage to function in the morning. Six days after withdrawing in Pensacola, he showed up at La Costa. Despite a wobbly 75 on the first day, he finished third on Sunday. Considering the strong field, and the $12,000 check he cashed, it was his best performance of the year. Then it was on to a grueling six tournaments in seven weeks. While Nicklaus carefully tended his game, gently polishing here and there, Trevino pounded on his like a blacksmith at the anvil.

It seemed to work. After the Tournament of Champions Trevino played well in Dallas, and he finally grabbed his first victory of the season, and a kiss from tournament sponsor Danny Thomas, in Memphis.

In Tennessee, Trevino had shown the strain of his punishing schedule. On Saturday he had been poised over a short par putt on the eighteenth green when Arnold Palmer, playing in the fairway on the same hole, cracked a four wood. To

Palmer's surprise, the ball reached the green, rolling to a stop near Trevino. The shot brought a roar from the huge crowd at greenside and Trevino missed his putt. Palmer was apologetic. Trevino was apoplectic. After turning in his scorecard, he had the police help him push through the crowd and left the course without signing a single autograph or answering a single reporter's question.

All of Saturday's turmoil was erased on Sunday. Wielding a new putter, Trevino rolled in four long birdie putts ranging from twelve to forty feet. Though he didn't look at the scoreboard once, by the middle of his round he was certain he had taken the lead. In the end he set a tournament record of 67 and won the $35,000 first prize. Two weeks later, at the Kemper Open in Charlotte, North Carolina, he collected another $20,000 for finishing second.

If, after Charlotte, Trevino had gone home to El Paso, he would have been able to rest and practice in peace, and then proceed west for the U.S. Open. Memphis and Charlotte had restored his competitive edge, his putting stroke, and his confidence. They had also vaulted him past the $100,000 mark in earnings, all the way to second place on the money list.

But second to Nicklaus was not enough for the ex-caddie from Tenison Park. He wanted more, and so with the Open a week away, he went on to Philadelphia and a tournament where half the players weren't even eligible for the U.S. Open. The pickings looked easy, and he wanted some.

If the fact that all his main competitors had skipped Philly didn't tell Trevino something, the headache, fever, and hacking cough he brought there should have. In grinding his way through so many events, applying ever more pressure to himself, Trevino had literally made himself sick. He completed one round and finally saw a doctor. He had pneumonia and a sinus infection. The next day he was in Providence Memorial Hospital in El Paso.

While the defending champion Trevino would approach the Open not knowing if he could even compete, Arnold Palmer faced the challenge of another Major at a time when his game was in decline, and the pressure of his outside interests were never greater. Although Nicklaus would one day build a comparable empire, in 1972 the undisputed leader in off-the-course business interests was Palmer. In fact, no one in all of sports—not Joe Namath or Mickey Mantle or Wilt Chamberlain—could match him in wealth or business prowess.

Beginning in the late 1950s, when he agreed to pitch Coke and L&M cigarettes (two products to which he was firmly addicted), Palmer had accepted an array of endorsement deals that brought him millions of dollars per year from manufacturers of everything from catsup to tractors. He licensed wallpaper, cookware, even Japanese tearooms. At the peak of this activity, in the late 1960s and early 1970s, a Palmer fan could wear Palmer-endorsed suits, drive a Palmer-backed Lincoln, maintain it with Palmer-certified Pennzoil, and watch a TV with a screen so sturdy that ol' Arnie couldn't drive a golf ball through it. (At least that's what the TV commercials showed.)

All of this was arranged by agent Mark McCormack, who had the wisdom to sell the Palmer personality and the values he represented—daring, strength, courage, integrity—rather than his status as a tournament winner. Of course, this couldn't have been possible if Palmer hadn't been a winner in the first place. But in avoiding advertisements that featured his man holding a trophy, McCormack protected Palmer's value for the day when someone else held the prizes.

In addition to all the endorsement deals, a company called Arnold Palmer Enterprises owned and operated a string of its own businesses, including a golf club manufacturer, a course design company, and a chain of more than one hundred dry cleaners. Partnerships with other companies produced a highly successful line of clothing that sold worldwide.

With these vast and varied interests came such a tight and intense schedule that Palmer's golf must have been compromised. It would be impossible to say whether he may have won more tournaments, and more Majors, given a looser set of commitments. But he would eventually admit that there were times that it was convenient to have these demands as an excuse as his play began to suffer.

As Tour '72 turned toward the U.S. Open, Palmer's play was clearly suffering. He had posted too many scores in the 80s, and too few in the 60s. Given his age, it was reasonable to wonder if his winning days were over. Given his connection to millions of fans, many of whom felt they actually knew him, Palmer had to answer questions about his future wherever he went.

A few weeks after the Masters he appeared at a golf course in Leesburg, Virginia, to help raise money for a local charity. Well over a thousand people turned out, and when a few got the chance to ask the King some questions, they inevitably asked what ailed his game.

Palmer revealed that he had put extra pressure on himself

and had pushed his practice and playing time before the Masters. As a result, "My game fell apart after the first day." For the rest of the season, he promised, he would play only in premier events and save his best for the Majors.

"I suppose it's inevitable that I'll quit the tour someday," he allowed, "but I hope it isn't for a long while." He wouldn't go any further on the question of his future, but when asked about Nicklaus and the Slam, he couldn't help but be a bit more definitive. He said he wasn't convinced that Nicklaus could do it.

By mid-May of 1972, Arnold Palmer wouldn't even rank in the top twenty on the money list. Like many people his age, Palmer found his eyesight was giving him trouble, and he tried both contact lenses and regular glasses—sometimes in the same round of golf—to no avail. Vision problems may well have affected his putting. At almost every tournament the local paper would print at least one photo of him grimacing as his ball failed to drop. He gamely promised to play better each week, but then found himself struggling to explain high scores.

In the weeks before the U.S. Open, his best finish was sixth at the Byron Nelson Classic in Dallas. Even there, at a moment when he could have won with a Sunday charge, he faltered with three-putt bogeys on two of the final four holes. The next week, at the Danny Thomas–Memphis Open, Palmer was helped by a little boy who kicked his ball out of the rough and onto the eighth green. The stroke this boy saved put Arnie in tenth place but didn't boost his winnings enough to cover the cost of a $1,200 watch he lost somewhere on the grounds of the golf course.

Heading to Pebble Beach in the middle of June, Palmer

had won a scant $41,331 in the year and had lost even more ground to the players at the top of the PGA Tour money list. Gary Player, who had been abroad more weeks than he had been in the States, was well ahead of Palmer in earnings; so were little-known competitors like Paul Harney, Lou Graham, and Bob Murphy. At the top of the list, Jack Nicklaus had won almost four times as much as Palmer, playing in many fewer events. Rarely in the ten years they had competed on the tour had either man been so far ahead of the other.

With so much uncertainty surrounding them, Trevino, Player, and Palmer didn't seem to present much of a challenge as Nicklaus approached the second leg of the Grand Slam. In almost every newspaper in America, the sportswriters made him the favorite. The *Atlanta Constitution* declared it the "Year of Nicklaus." The *New York Times* invited renowned golf architect Robert Trent Jones to examine the courses and assess Nicklaus's chances. He began by saying, "You realize if you talked about anyone else winning the Grand Slam you would be ridiculed?" He then went on to make it seem quite likely that Nicklaus would win at Pebble Beach and Muirfield. He made it seem as if Oakland Hills, where the fourth Major would be played, presented the only real challenge to the world's greatest player. (Trent Jones had redesigned the course himself in 1951, making it one of the toughest in the world.) But how much of a challenge could Oakland Hills be, when as a mere twenty-year-old amateur Nicklaus had finished fourth the last time a Major was played there?

A speculative frenzy began to build around Nicklaus, and

he was the object of rampant betting and debate in clubhouses around the country. His Grand Slam chase drew even more attention than it may have otherwise because sports fans were disillusioned with the object of their usual summer affections: baseball. Deprived of it by the strike, people had discovered that they could get along without the game, and many found themselves captivated, for the first time, by golf's superstars and the Slam. The high TV ratings for golf broadcasts suggested this, and more proof arrived when the strike ended. At ballparks around the country, attendance was low, and stayed low, and many of those who did go to the games booed both the players and the owners.

Outside of sports, America was captivated by a new TV series and an epic feature film, each of which reflected the gritty reality of the times. On March 15, Francis Ford Coppola's *The Godfather* premiered in New York. Pauline Kael noted that it brought "tragic realism" to filmmaking. *The Godfather* became a landmark moment in art and shaped the work of an entire generation of auteurs. Just as influential, in its own medium, was the new TV series *All in the Family*, which swept the Emmy Awards in 1972. For the first time, a comic series focused on a less-than-idealized American family. It dealt with the same serious issues—race, the Vietnam War, feminism— that troubled its audience.

In the harsh, real world, Americans found confusion and fear. Though the North Vietnamese Easter Offensive was being slowed, Americans were shocked by reports that even as U.S. advisers tried to rally them, Southern troops were literally running past their officers in panicked retreat. Around the country, tens of thousands marched in major cities to protest the war. Despite the opposition, the president ordered increased bombing of North Vietnam.

In California, self-proclaimed communist and former University of California professor Angela Davis was found not guilty on charges that she had participated in murder, kidnapping, and conspiracy in connection with attempts to free imprisoned members of the Black Panther Party. The verdict was decried by Davis's many critics, but it did put the lie to her claim that a black militant couldn't get a fair trial in the United States.

Finally, in a tragic reprise of the political violence that had already claimed three national figures, presidential candidate George Wallace was attacked by a would-be assassin in a shopping-center parking lot in Laurel, Maryland. Though he would survive, the Alabama governor would spend the rest of his life a wheelchair-bound paraplegic.

CHAPTER 5

Nobody ever wins the Open.
Everyone else always loses it.
—Bobby Jones

A full eight days before the U.S. Open was to begin, as Lee Trevino came down with pneumonia in Philadelphia, Jack Nicklaus was on the Pebble Beach Golf Links, testing the turf, the winds, the angles. He had played Pebble's eighteen scenically breathtaking holes perhaps a hundred times before. In 1961 he won the U.S. Amateur Championship there, and he won the Crosby tournament in both 1967 and earlier in 1972. But he had played the course under summer conditions only a few times. And he had never seen it prepared in the way the United States Golf Association readies a course—deeper rough, faster greens, extra bunkers—for its annual torture test.

By 1972, Jack Nicklaus had already built an imposing record in the U.S. Open, which had become the most prestigious event in golf. He played in it for the first time at age seventeen, and missed the cut. But three years later, in 1960, he posted the lowest score ever made by an amateur—282—and had a chance to win on a final day when Gene Littler defeated Arnold Palmer. In 1962, Nicklaus did win, beating Palmer in a play-off to become the youngest champion since Bobby Jones in 1923. Nicklaus won the Open again in 1967, and could claim three more finishes in the top three.

An early arrival at any Open site is a big advantage. During the official practice rounds held in the few days before competition, golfers are permitted to play the course only under the rules of regular tournament rounds. This means no extra putting on the greens, no test shots from the fairways, no practice in the bunkers. But in the week before the tournament, Nicklaus could do almost anything he wanted. With his ten-year-old son Jackie and caddie Angelo Argea in tow, he picked out five or six holes at a time and worked them over like a detective at a crime scene. He hit drives from different spots on the teeing areas and second shots from various places in the fairways and rough. He tested bunkers—new, soft sand had been installed—and greens, and chipped from every imaginable position. In this way he achieved what he later termed a kind of "intimacy" with the course.

It was fortunate for Nicklaus that he was blessed with the wealth that made it easy to skip twenty or more tournaments per year and devote long stretches of time to preparing for each Major. He was sometimes criticized for taking such long breaks from the regular tour and depriving sponsors of the gate receipts his entry could generate. But from the very beginning of his career Nicklaus had been driven by his desire to make his mark on golf history by winning Majors. This had led him to develop a very deliberate and self-indulgent method of preparing himself for these four peak moments in each year. No matter what it required, Jack Nicklaus would make himself happy, healthy, and confident when his name was called on the first tee for every Masters, U.S. Open, British Open, and PGA Championship he entered.

Most pros would have had to sacrifice something significant to prepare in a similar way. Buddy Allin, the Vietnam vet, would have had to skip a couple of weeks' work on the regular tour and shoulder the expense of camping out on the Monterey Peninsula. But as number fifty-three on the money list, with barely $17,000 earned for the year, how could he justify missing paychecks when a few hundred here and there bought diapers for his son Aaron and gas to keep the Gremlin on the road? Besides, he was realistic about his chances. Two weeks or two months on the Pebble Beach course wouldn't guarantee Allin a victory in the Open. The same was true for a hundred others who would compete in the event. Granted, they had a chance to win if somehow they played better than they had in their lives for four straight days. But that would require magic, or divine intervention, not practice.

This is why the Nicklaus method was for those at the top who played a game apart, where maximum effort could yield the stroke or two that would bring victory. With nineteen Opens behind him, Arnold Palmer was of this rank, and he quietly joined Nicklaus at Pebble Beach in the week before the tournament began. Like Nicklaus, Palmer came to experiment and to test the course and his game under the conditions that summertime and the USGA created. He had another goal, one he never mentioned openly, but which was the most important. He had gone to Pebble early, looking for the flame of desire.

Publicly Palmer maintained his optimism. "I can win it," he said bluntly. And on the course he was his usual upbeat self. He even played one entire practice round with a flower—a gift from a young woman—tucked behind his ear.

But privately, the doubts loomed large. Palmer had last won the Open in 1960. Since then, he had lost three play-offs and finished third once. This year, his seventeenth year on the PGA Tour, Palmer had no victories in a dozen tries. His army, loyal but ever attuned to its leader, had begun to lose faith. And Palmer knew that when he got into trouble on the course they no longer expected a miracle. Instead, they worried and hoped and even prayed he would recover.

Though he hadn't mentioned it to anyone, Palmer was feeling his age. His legs were not as strong as they once were. He was losing the ability to focus intently over four full days of play. And worst of all, he had noticed that his appetite for winning was fading. To compensate, Palmer had cut back on his consumption of alcohol—he was a prodigious drinker—and increased his sleep. He wasn't sure this would help, but it was worth a try.

"I have never not enjoyed the competition, or playing," said Palmer, thirty years later. "But at that time I was disappointed that my closing wasn't as good. Psychologically, I just couldn't finish the tournaments the same way. You can't explain it, but it's why, if you look at the statistics, very few people are shining stars past forty. You have to remember, I was twenty-five when I went out there in 1955. I considered myself pretty competitive for twenty years, but by 1970, '71, '72 there was a drop-off."

Along with the growing feeling that his best days were over, Palmer also kept secret the seriousness of his eye trouble. At his annual eye exam, done in May, his doctor had confirmed that the nearsightedness Palmer had struggled with since the season began was getting worse. For his entire career he had enjoyed perfect vision. Now he had trouble judging distances on the course and following the ball into the sky. If he used lenses to fix these problems, then focusing on the ball at address became uncomfortable.

"It was very frustrating," added Palmer. Though the press took notice of his continuing struggle to find the right glasses or contact lenses, he didn't want his competitors to know how much he was affected. In fact, "it was the most traumatic thing that happened in my career."

In contrast, Lee Trevino's health problems could hardly be called traumatic, or career-threatening. Actually, they could be considered ironic. In January he had laughingly predicted that he would spend a lazy week in bed to prepare for the defense of his U.S. Open title. Now he was actually doing just that.

Of course, there was nothing funny in the fact that in pushing himself too hard, and ignoring his milder symptoms, Trevino had put himself in danger of missing the Open entirely. Fearing he would relapse, or develop serious complications, his doctors said that their pneumonia-stricken patient would not be discharged until Wednesday, which would make an appearance at Pebble Beach Thursday almost impossible. They pumped him full of medicines and warned him that he might not get any closer to the tournament than any of the millions who would watch it on television.

Faced with being the first U.S. Open champ to miss defending his title since 1949, when Ben Hogan almost died in a car crash, Trevino wouldn't accept the doctors' prognosis. He insisted he would walk out of Providence Hospital on Tuesday and make his Thursday starting time in California. Unable to practice, he exercised with a spring device and put weights on his legs, hoping that as he moved around in his bed, the extra effort required would prevent his muscles from atrophying.

When he was supposed to lie still, Trevino took up a little yellow notepad and pencils and began sketching every hole on the course from memory. While Nicklaus and Palmer were actually making practice shots from every possible spot, Trevino colored in the greens and red flags, the practice green, and even the clubhouse. He then imagined playing the course, and drew lines to show where he might send each shot.

Though his doctors kept admonishing him to rest, Trevino used a positive X-ray reading—his lungs were clearing—as justification for a little putting practice. He had a putter and a few balls brought to the hospital, and when the ward grew quiet in the early hours of the morning, he practiced his stroke on a putting carpet he unrolled in front of his bed.

On the Monday before the start of the Open, bedridden Lee Trevino clowned for a photographer, opening wide as his wife, Claudia, approached with an atomizer filled with medicine. He said Nicklaus risked his game getting "stale" from too much practice. And he reminded the reporters who visited that he wouldn't have spent extra time on the Open course even if he had been healthy. "I never worry about the next tournament, no matter what it is, until I'm through with the one I'm playing," he insisted. He also challenged conventional wisdom about Nicklaus dominating at Pebble Beach. "I *can* beat him. I'm *gonna* beat him," he added, sounding a bit like Muhammad Ali. "You gotta hit it straight there and I can hit straight as anybody."

The next day, looking somewhat paler and thinner than usual, Trevino checked himself out of the hospital. He headed straight for the El Paso Country Club, stopping only long enough to tell reporters, in a hoarse voice, "I feel so good I could jump in the ring with Joe Frazier." At the club he played eighteen holes, putting so well that he made five birdies and an eagle to score 65.

During his Wednesday morning flight to San Francisco, Trevino felt strangely confident. As he had lain in bed, sketching away, he had understood that the keys to playing well at Pebble Beach under U.S. Open conditions would be straight driving, avoiding the rough, and deft putting. Trevino knew he hit his driver straight, and that a week of extra practice wouldn't have helped much there. And his putting had been improving in the weeks before he was hospitalized. He had reason to hope the stroke was still there.

After a quiet arrival at the Pebble Beach course, Trevino hung around the first tee until he could join a group for a practice round. While on the course he coughed and sniffed and honked. The defending Open champion was followed by a large gallery, who watched him score a two-over-par 74. His most eventful hole was number twelve, a par three, where he hit a tree, watched the ball ricochet onto the green, and then sank a twenty-footer for birdie. Afterward he said he still felt sick, but that a few breaks like the one he caught at the twelfth would likely revive him.

Trevino accepted that despite his status as the defending champ, Nicklaus was the one everyone expected to win. In every pre-tournament review, the press named Nicklaus the favorite, predicting he would reach the halfway mark in the Grand Slam campaign on Sunday afternoon with a score near par.

The only one to get prickly in his response to these predictions was Gary Player, who arrived just a few days before the tournament to find that Nicklaus was on everyone's mind. "Jack is good, but I'm never afraid of him," he snapped. "I've beaten him head-to-head in the World Match Play the last two times. I wouldn't be here if I were afraid of him." The outburst was uncharacteristic and may have been sharpened by the pain Player was feeling in his abdomen. He was silently suffering with a blocked ureter, which would be diagnosed and treated after the tournament.

As they arose on Thursday morning, each of the 150 men who would play in the 1972 U.S. Open understood that their two most imposing opponents were not Nicklaus and Trevino but rather the course itself and the tournament's traditions. It is tradition for the USGA's officials to select one of the country's—and therefore the world's—toughest courses for its annual championship and then fiddle with it to make it so difficult that they squeeze howls of complaint out of a few of the competitors.

The Pebble Beach Golf Links was made for the Open. Built in 1918 to serve both the public and guests at the Del Monte Lodge Hotel, the course is known for its long, difficult par fours, small greens, and myriad opportunities for losing a ball in the ocean or the sand. Though often overlooked, the difficulty of the greens at Pebble could not be overstated. They were small even for the era when they were built. And their contours were hard to read. In some cases putts at Pebble break *away* from the ocean, which is the opposite of what is expected. Sometimes putts on these greens even appear to turn uphill, in defiance of gravity.

The weather on the Monterey Peninsula, as variable as the climate on the Scottish coast, presents additional problems. A gray and foggy morning with barely a breeze can be followed by a sunny, windswept afternoon. The wind can affect every shot. When it is calm, the 110-yard par-three seventh hole can be reached with a pitching iron. When it blows hard, a long iron or wood might be required.

Even the weeds at Pebble Beach present an unusual challenge. A pale green, sand-loving thing called the ice plant (*Mesembryanthemum crystallinium*) grows along the oceanside fairways. A succulent, its translucent fingers seem to grab at a player's club as it approaches the ball. Sometimes a fiercely struck wedge will get a trapped ball out. But even pros can have trouble doing this with a single swing.

To add to the everyday challenges of the course, the USGA built five new bunkers, locating four of them near spots where hard-hitting pros would likely land their drives. Fresh, fluffy Pacific Coast beach sand was trucked in and dumped in those and the rest of the sand traps, ensuring that balls would bury if they landed with full force. New tees were built on holes number three and ten, adding fifteen yards to each. The extra distance would be especially bothersome on three, where the change made it that much harder for players to clear a ravine between the teeing ground and the fairway. On almost every hole, the grass on the flanks of the fairways was allowed to grow extra long to create truly penal rough.

As usual, the USGA wanted fast, smooth greens. But as had happened at Augusta, ragged *poa annua* had invaded the Pebble Beach greens. To combat this weed's tendency to grow tufted and leggy, the greens were rolled and cut to three thirty-seconds of an inch, half their regular height. The players weren't the only ones upset by this shaving, which caused some patches of brown to appear. Greenkeeper Roger Larson was so alarmed by the trimming that he ordered heavy watering, day and night, to keep the grass from dying.

Though many grumbled about the conditions, only one player spoke loudly. Frank Beard, a thirty-two-year-old with ten years on tour, spoke what, to Pebble's purists, were blasphemous words. "It's a good golf course, not a great one," said Beard, arguing that if so much effort had been needed to make Pebble more severe, perhaps it was unworthy to begin with. "I think Augusta National is a great course and so is Hilton Head," he said. "They don't have a lot of rough to trick them up."

The criticism shocked some, and Beard would be subjected to catcalls and even booing when he finally teed up his ball to play. But anyone who knew him understood that Beard was a serious man, more thoughtful and more successful than the average pro golfer. He had ten wins to his credit, including two at the prestigious Tournament of Champions. The leading money winner in 1969, he had come close to winning the Open in 1965.

Despite his success, Beard harbored a level of insecurity more common to the lower-ranked players. In retirement he would confess that he had suffered from a crippling sort of perfectionism that left him submerged in shame if he performed badly. Unlike Palmer, whom he described as "a child at play," Beard was a stressed-out adult who especially dreaded going to the golf course when he had a chance to win. These feelings caused Beard to be more keenly resentful of any effort the USGA exerted to make the ordinary competitor even more miserable at the Open. He didn't need the extra stress.

The resentments of one player would never be enough to sway the officials of the USGA to loosen any of the screws it had turned tight at Pebble. But when Nicklaus and others privately expressed the same concerns that Beard made public, their words had some effect. Before the Thursday round came an announcement that two adjustments would be made. First, a layer of sand would be removed from a bunker on the fifth hole, so balls wouldn't bury so deeply. Second, some rough would be cut down to widen the fairway on the eighth hole. One of the most dramatic par fours in the world, number eight at Pebble required a blind uphill drive followed by a long approach shot across an inlet to a small green. For the Open, the fairway had been pinched to twenty-six yards of width. Now a strip four yards wide would be cut shorter on the right side, offering players a little more safety on their drives.

The changes made by the USGA's officials amounted to

an admission that they had gone too far. But they weren't enough to save Frank Beard from opening with an 85, following that with an 80, and missing the cut. He lost the Open, but he won the unspoken gratitude of at least a few of the 149 other men who, partly due to his outspokenness, had felt the pressure ease just a bit.

Pressure was the likely culprit in the demise of one of the early leaders on opening day. Homero Blancas, who had won the Phoenix Open early in the year, made four birdies on the first five holes, only to score a double bogey on the next hole and a triple on the sixteenth. (He hit his ball out of bounds there.) Playing just ahead of Nicklaus, Blancas went from runaway leader to a 74. But the twist in his adventure story was not how far he fell from the lead but how close he remained at the end of the day. Seventy-four, it would turn out, was a very good score on the first day of the 1972 U.S. Open.

Adhering to the Bobby Jones aphorism about everyone losing the Open, dozens and dozens of the world's best golfers went out on an extraordinarily calm, clear, and temperate day and posted some of the worst scores in their careers. Seals chased fish in the becalmed red kelp beds just off the oceanside holes while 140 of the 150 contestants failed to break par. (Nearly a third of the field—forty-eight players to be exact—couldn't break 80 on this day.) As Gary Player would confirm on the course, and in his complaints afterward, the powdery-fine silica in the bunkers confounded almost everyone, with the exception of Nicklaus, who had practiced in them over and over again.

Gary Player had more reason than most to be annoyed, if not with the course, then with himself. A chip to within inches of the hole, and two long birdie putts, had brought him to the fifteenth tee a full three strokes under par and poised to end the day alone in first position. Then on fifteen, a run-in with a bunker left him wounded with a bogey. He made another bogey on the following hole and then—perhaps it was frustration—he failed to exercise proper caution on seventeen. Hoping to get the ball close to the pin, he chose a three wood for his approach and almost sent the ball into Monterey Bay.

Despite all his meandering, at day's end Player's simple score of even par left him within a single shot of the leaders, who included Nicklaus and the 1969 Open winner, Orville Moody. A chunky, red-haired Oklahoman with muttonchop sideburns, Moody had played with Trevino in the Army, where he rose to oversee all the service's golf courses world-wide. He had joined the tour in 1967. Though it won him instant fame, Moody's U.S. Open victory would ultimately do him more harm than good. In the uproar that followed, his marriage ended and his game deteriorated. When he finally left the tour, in the early 1980s, the 1969 U.S. Open would stand as his only victory.

At the 1972 Open, Moody appeared wearing a surgical mask, which he hoped would filter some of the pollen that caused him serve allergy attacks. A 77 in the second round would begin his slide away from the leaders. "I was happier when I was in the Army," he said during the tournament.

In scoring one under par on opening day, Jack Nicklaus followed a strategy he had settled on during his preparations. He wanted to start carefully, avoiding the kind of first-day disaster—like Homero Blancas's triple bogey—that can be so demoralizing. For this reason, he chose not to go for the green with his second shot on the par-five eighteenth hole, even though his drive had put him in position to do so. (A long, curving hole, the eighteenth has the ocean to its left and out of bounds on the right. It is one of the most dramatic finishing holes in the world.)

Nicklaus was also aware of the dangers of being overly cautious, so he took calculated risks when the odds were in his favor. With the greens playing a bit softer than most players expected, he tried to land his ball close to the pins. The results—fifteen quiet pars, two routine birdies, one three-putt bogey—produced the 71 that was good enough for the lead.

In many other tournaments, scores much higher than Nicklaus's would have pushed players toward the cutline, but at this U.S. Open anything around a 75 left a competitor in contention. In fact, the first-day scores in the 1972 tournament were among the highest ever recorded in the seventy-seven times the event had been played. As they came off the eighteenth green, one weary soul after another had a sad tale to tell.

After achieving a remarkable three under par in just eight holes, Jim Weichers got tangled in the ice plants along the ninth, scored a triple bogey, and then finished with a 74.

On the fifth tee, Bunky Henry was comfortably one under par. He finished with a day's-high 88. Henry was so confounded that when his ball landed within twelve feet of the cup on the eighteenth hole, he asked playing partner Deane Beman for odds on his making a routine two-putt par. Beman declined to speculate. Henry made bogey.

At the end of his round, Jim Jamieson wrote 82 on his card and, laughing, asked the USGA officials if he and his playing partners, Frank Beard and Al Geiberger, could submit a "best ball" score.

Tony Jacklin's 75 was notable for the fact that it included two double bogeys. One of these came after he landed his approach shot just eighteen feet from the hole on number ten. Four putts later, he had a score of six. After his round, Jacklin compared his experience to being a target in a shooting gallery. "I was in a daze," he said. "I didn't know what happened until three holes later."

If anyone had the right to feel dazed and to stumble around a bit, it was the defending champion. Lee Trevino had made sure to say that his very appearance at the Open was remarkable. "There's fourteen million people that know I just got out of the hospital, fourteen million that don't expect me to win," he croaked on the day he arrived at Pebble Beach. "If I shoot eight-five tomorrow they've expected it, so I've got no pressure."

This was standard Trevino pregame talk. Before important tournaments his ever-moving mouth first issued brave predictions of victory and then, as tee-off got closer, he claimed the underdog's status. If he could use Nicklaus, an illness, or any other factor to lower expectations, and perhaps lull his opponents, he did it. Years later he would admit that the real purpose was not to psych out anyone else, but to prepare himself to perform confidently. If he also happened to bring fans into his cause, all the better.

Playing in the sunshine that arrived in midmorning, Trevino was accompanied by about 1,000 of the 14,000 people who turned out for the first day of competition. His weakened condition showed. A few of his long iron shots fell short, mostly because of fatigue and a loss of muscle tone in the lower half of his body. On the long par-five fourteenth hole, he hit a near-perfect drive but almost missed the ball entirely with his subsequent iron shot. He was fortunate to avoid a bogey.

When it was over, Trevino wobbled up to the clubhouse, where he would chat with reporters for a few moments. (Afterward he would collapse in his room in the Del Monte Lodge and sleep for twenty hours.) Trevino had a little trouble recalling what had just transpired. "I don't know," he said, "I'm lucky I finished." He did more than just finish. His score, a 74, was better than most, including the 77 posted by Arnold Palmer, who began the day with bogeys on the first three holes.

With eight long years between him and his last Major win, Arnold Palmer awoke Friday morning to the likely prospect that he could be sent home before the real contest—the weekend rounds—even began. (Leaving a Major at the midpoint is a miserable thing, even when you're flying your own airplane.) The wind had picked up. The greens had dried out. Nothing in the conditions suggested Pebble would play any easier than it had the day before. But Palmer believed he could go out and do something no one had done yet this week— break 70.

Palmer began his Friday assault on the course in the way he had said it must be done, by covering the first six holes—the least difficult stretch—in two under par. If he had just played steady par into the clubhouse he would have beaten the low mark set by Nicklaus the day before. But on number eight he three-putted from a mere twenty-five feet after navigating to the green. At that moment, he felt as angry as he had ever felt on a golf course. But the heat of his temper reignited his competitive flame.

Dressed in bright plaid pants, cardigan sweater, and a shirt with a wide flapping collar, Palmer prowled the fairway with a style and aggression reminiscent of 1960. He won the Open that year with a powerful display of golf on the final day that began with him reaching the first hole, a par four, with a 370-yard drive. This time, at Pebble, Palmer succeeded with both power and putting. With an eye on the scoreboard, he played the back nine in fewer strokes than anyone, rolling in mid-range putts for birdies at ten, twelve, seventeen, and eighteen. For a time on the back nine he was so pumped up by the crowd and his own performance that he had to consciously slow his swing to compensate for the adrenaline.

After six birdies and two bogeys, Palmer's scorecard read 68 when he signed it. At first he declared it his best round of the year, and then, gripped by his tendency toward hyperbole, he wondered aloud whether it may have been his best ever, better even than the 65 he shot while winning the Open in 1960. This speculation made more sense than it first seemed, because the conditions at Pebble Beach were, some would eventually say, the toughest ever at the national championship. An under-par round could only be achieved with consistent, excellent play, and Palmer had done just that over the entire course.

Palmer's number was matched only by a twenty-two-year-old rookie named Lanny Wadkins. Young Wadkins, who had attended Wake Forest University on an Arnold Palmer scholarship, would fade with weekend scores of 79 and 81. But he had shown the talent that would eventually win him the 1977 PGA Championship on this very course.

At the end of the day on Friday, at least, Wadkins found himself tied for the lead, and Palmer was just a single stroke back. This was because Jack Nicklaus had been blown off the course he had established the day before. Beginning with a bogey on the first hole, Nicklaus had scratched his way to two-under on the front nine. But on the back he had stumbled in an uncharacteristic way, posting three bogeys in a row.

The trouble had started when Nicklaus hit his ball out of bounds on the longest hole, par-five number fourteen, where his length was normally an advantage. Nicklaus was able to save himself from a double or triple bogey by making a twenty-six-foot putt, one of the longest anyone would make all week.

On the very next hole, a sudden wind literally knocked Nicklaus off balance as he was putting for par. He actually topped the ball, and it didn't come close to the hole. Then on sixteen he missed the green and had to scramble for bogey again.

In shooting 73 and failing to match his rather modest performance in the opening round, Nicklaus had allowed a dangerous assortment of challengers to creep close. Besides Palmer and Wadkins, the top ten, all within two strokes, included both Gary Player and Lee Trevino. Trevino had played as if he had come straight from Lourdes. In a performance overshadowed by Palmer's 68, he had snuffled his way to a 72. He had played himself into contention the way he said he would, hitting the ball so straight that he had driven into the rough just once in thirty-six holes.

Tied with Trevino was Lee Elder, whose scores of 75 and 71 had the media speculating again about the Masters. Under the new Masters entry rules, a top-sixteen performance at the U.S. Open meant an automatic invitation to Augusta. In the locker room reporters flocked around Elder. If he could only hold steady, he would make it for sure, he agreed. Unfortunately, Pebble Beach would get the best of Elder. Over the weekend he would struggle to a 79 and then an 80. He would miss a tie for sixteenth and lose his ticket to Augusta by three strokes.

Elder was not the only one to know U.S. Open pain. Arnold Palmer, who played with Elder on Saturday, had an unmatched record of suffering at the national championship. In 1966, at the tournament played at the Olympic Club in San Francisco, Palmer moved into the lead on the second round and widened his advantage to three shots by Sunday morning. On Sunday he teed off with his nearest challenger, Billy Casper, and roared to a 32 on the front nine, a pace that suggested he might break Ben Hogan's record for the lowest total—276—in the tournament's history. Casper, perhaps the best putter on tour, was not known for final-day charges, and with Palmer ahead by seven at the turn, even he seemed to accept that Palmer was playing for posterity. In his 1999 autobiography Palmer quoted a telling exchange he had with Casper on the tenth fairway.

"I'm going to have to go just to get second," said Casper, who was wary of those behind him.

"Don't worry, Bill," answered Palmer. "You'll finish second."

What happened in the next two hours would go down in history as the worst collapse ever seen in the modern era of the national championship. Having decided to ignore Casper, Palmer tried to best Hogan's record for lowest Open score. This approach netted an immediate bogey on ten, a birdie on twelve, and another bogey on thirteen. Remarkably enough, Palmer would still have surpassed Hogan with pars into the clubhouse. But instead he tried to extend his lead by shooting for the pin on the par-three fifteenth hole. The ball found a bunker. Palmer bogeyed. Casper made par. The gap between them fell to three strokes.

Suddenly aware that he should be fighting Casper rather than the record book, Palmer became irritated by the way his opponent's conservative play was being rewarded by the gods of golf. He responded in a way that was both true to his nature and disastrous. The next hole was a 604-yard monster that he tried to tame. His drive hooked into the rough. His second shot, a three iron, squirted across the fairway. Forced to chip out, he then went for the green with a three wood. It landed in a bunker and Palmer got up-and-down for a bogey six. As Casper rolled in a birdie putt, Palmer's head felt like it was going to explode.

By the time he reached the last hole, Palmer's lead was gone and his mind was reeling. He looked in the gallery for his wife, Winnie, but could not find her reassuring face. He thought about what his father had taught him about a slow backswing and keeping his body still to make a solid contact. He made par, but so did Casper, who then won it all the next day in a play-off. It was Palmer's third play-off loss in the Open.

The weight of so many disappointments had its effect on Palmer. Ever since that tournament at Olympic he almost always saw sympathy joined with the admiration in the faces of his fans and close supporters. But long after he had come to accept that his powers were waning, soldiers in the army could not. On U.S. Open Saturday in 1972 they shouted encouragement from behind the ropes on every hole.

Palmer heard them, and tried to fulfill their dreams as well as his own. But on greens that had begun to die and were becoming rock hard, the putting stroke that had been a little better on Friday turned a little worse on Saturday. Using one of the 1,200 putters he had purchased over a lifetime pursuing the right "touch," Palmer missed seven birdie putts, including one that he left short from just four feet. In all, he would fail on thirteen putts of under twenty feet. On a practice green, most pros would sink half of them.

The shaky putting was a sign of Palmer's age, and so, too, was the failure of focus he experienced after four or five holes. He wasn't distracted, he just wasn't fully engaged as he stepped up to swing. The result was hesitation on club selection and an unusual sensitivity to movement and noise in the gallery. More than once he asked for marshals to quiet the crowd. They complied, but it didn't help much.

With all his struggle against the course, his swing, and his own mind, Palmer nevertheless managed to post a 73, which matched front-runner Nicklaus for the day and left him two strokes behind. For his part, Nicklaus had continued to play highly controlled golf against a course that would punish anything else. Having hooked his three wood on the first tee Thursday, he used a two iron to begin every round for the rest of the week, to good result. This disciplined approach helped Nicklaus to avoid disaster, but produced a mere seven birdies in three whole days of competition. No one was more surprised by the high scores than Nicklaus himself.

"I'd have said you were cracked if you told me I'd be leading with even par after three rounds," he said.

Each one of Nicklaus's birdies was a precious thing, but even more significant was the scrambling he did to save par over and over again. A perfect example came on the sixth hole, which begins the magnificent stretch of the course that follows the oceanside cliff. Playing from a tee set in a wooded area, Nicklaus hit his drive left, into a huge bunker. He found sand again on his second shot but managed to blast out and make par even though his ball never touched the grass before it reached the green.

The string of bunker play continued on the very next hole. Number seven at Pebble is a 122-yard par three that juts into the ocean and may well be the most well-known golf hole in the world. Here Nicklaus's tee shot was saved from tumbling down the cliff when it came to rest in the strip of sand that runs behind the green. A blast and two putts resulted in a bogey four.

In all, Nicklaus hit five bunkers on Saturday but lost only one stroke to par because of it. He made up for this error on the extra-long fourteenth, where he flung his bunkered ball to within five feet of the hole and rolled the putt in for birdie. For Nicklaus, whose only weakness was sand play, this was especially satisfying. For the rest of the field, most of whom hadn't enjoyed enough practice in the strange bunkers to master them, it was proof that his preparations were worthwhile.

As he worked the course, Nicklaus looked stronger and more confident than ever. With all the pudge of his early years gone and his sun-bleached blond hair blowing in the wind, he seemed completely at ease, even when studying greens that were, ultimately, impossible to read with any certainty. This was the difference that his preparation made. It showed most on the back nine, where the rest of the players just couldn't match Nicklaus's steady performance. After two days of play, the USGA issued a statistical report that said that in 300 rounds, the field had taken 527 more strokes on the back nine than on the front.

All day Saturday most of the men who had pursued Nicklaus in the early rounds faltered in the face of ever-stronger winds and ever-greater stress. Lanny Wadkins scored two double bogeys in a row on fifteen and sixteen en route to a 79. Homero Blancas made a double on ten in his round of 76.

One of the few who seemed unperturbed by the inward nine at Pebble was Nicklaus's nemesis, Trevino. Still weak and a bit glassy-eyed, Trevino chose longer clubs on many shots to compensate for his lack of strength. A good example of how well this strategy worked came on the seventeenth hole, a 218-yard par three. While other players hit irons, Trevino trusted the accuracy of his driver, and was rewarded. The ball curved onto the green, where he then made a twenty-five-footer for birdie.

Trevino putted extremely well. He guessed that it was because he felt completely relaxed. On the finishing hole he played to the crowd a bit as he made his birdie, staggered a bit, and then waved his hat to acknowledge the cheers.

On Saturday night, while Lee Trevino fell into the heavy sleep of a man dosed with antihistamines, Jack Nicklaus was restless. Awaking early, he tried to will himself back into slumber. But he made it only about halfway there, settling into a half-sleep state that produced what seemed like a hundred dreams of disaster on the finishing holes at Pebble Beach. He awoke feeling tired and agitated. It was no way to start the final day of play at the U.S. Open.

A look at the Sunday morning scoreboard explained why Nicklaus's subconscious had given him so much trouble. Besides Trevino, who was one stroke back, Nicklaus also faced a charged-up Palmer who burned to show he wasn't finished in the Majors. And though Gary Player was probably too far back in the pack to be a threat, a few capable competitors with no previous wins at Majors lurked a stroke or two behind. One was Tom Weiskopf, who had proven at Fort Lauderdale that he was not afraid to take on the Bear, the King, or any other superstar worthy of a nickname. Another was Bruce Crampton, an Australian with many years of experience who had played well enough at the Masters to tie for second. Blessed with one of the most graceful swings in golf, Crampton had quietly won nine times on tour and netted more than $1 million playing golf around the world. He and Weiskopf were both in the top ten on the money list before the U.S. Open began.

The Sunday gallery at Pebble Beach, and the millions in the national audience who would watch on TV, got what they wanted for the last day at the Open: a stage set for drama. The two greatest players in the game at the time, Nicklaus and Trevino, would be paired in the last group to tee off. Just ahead of them would be groups including Crampton, Weiskopf, and Palmer.

At noon Lee Trevino, wearing a red shirt, matching golf glove, and black sweater and pants, casually putted some golf balls on the practice green in front of the Del Monte Lodge. Having practically rolled back the stone and risen from the dead, he was in a spiritual sort of mood, so he delivered his version of a Sunday sermon to the sportswriters who gathered around. It was the kind of homily that could be uttered only by a man who had been amply blessed with tournament victories, or who felt completely right with Almighty God.

"The Man up there," he said, pointing to the sky, "has already decided who is going to win here, so it's no use getting all uptight about it." Then he paused, and smiled slightly. "I'm just worried. It's overcast, and I'm afraid He can't see me."

Besides God, Trevino said, a champion is defined by attitude. And the proper attitude involves accepting bad shots as part of the game and avoiding fits of temper. "There ain't no justice" in golf, he added, so there's no sense in looking for it.

From the putting green Trevino went to the practice tee, where he clowned a bit and amused a small crowd with his usual tricks. "Look at that," he called to Nicklaus after hitting several shots along the ground. "I can't get them up, Jack." Nicklaus smiled.

Though Nicklaus and Trevino would be the big draws for the day, a few hundred yards away, on the other side of the lodge, Arnold Palmer attracted a gallery like a magnet attracts iron filings. The army, swelled with new recruits, flanked the fairway on the first hole and roared with delight as he hit a near perfect shot to the green. This was followed by a collective sigh as Palmer missed the seven-foot putt for birdie. Still, there were no deserters as Palmer attacked, and attacked again, finally scoring a birdie on number three with a long, long putt. Though he felt encouraged, Palmer recognized that the course was the toughest he had ever seen in the U.S. Open. He knew better than anyone in the gallery that the only way he would win it would be if Nicklaus lost it.

It was 1 P.M. when a cheer announced that Palmer had shaved the difference between himself and Nicklaus to a single stroke. Nicklaus approached the first green, felt the strong breeze, and began to think that the scores would be very high this day. The biggest problem was the wind, which was gusting harder than it had on any previous day, reaching thirty miles per hour at times. It was so powerful that a sailing regatta planned for Monterey Bay had been canceled. Only a few boats could be seen dodging whitecaps at midday, their canvases stretched taut.

Up on land, the onshore winds whipped the yellow flags that marked the holes and buffeted the players and their shots. On some holes the wind would change direction once or twice, disappear, and then blow again in the brief moment a player stood contemplating his options. A club chosen to compensate for a stiff headwind could easily send a ball screaming over the green because the breeze just happened to die down for a second or two.

The breeze also dried out the greens, the way it will dry a person's unprotected skin. Already baked by the sun, and weakened by the USGA's triple cutting, these normally lush, receptive landing areas became as hard and smooth as kitchen-floor linoleum. Blade by blade, the grass was dying. Not even the highest, most softly struck shot would hold. As patches turned brown, they created new breaks in the putting surface. By the time the last pair—Nicklaus and Trevino—reached each hole, more than seventy players had already worked them over. As he first observed their condition, Nicklaus decided that they were so bad, he might not even need to make par to win.

Despite his cheeriness and faith, Lee Trevino was destined to run out of the adrenaline, or nerve, or whatever it was that had powered him through the previous three days of golf. He made the sign of the cross, hit his drive, and like Nicklaus parred the first hole. But then he scored bogeys on three of the next five holes. The putt that seemed to signal the end of the round came on the sixth, where he slid a three-footer past the hole. Weary and at last out of luck, Trevino would card a 78, a full seven strokes worse than he had scored the day before.

A birdie on number two restored Nicklaus's lead on Palmer. He then increased it on Pebble's signature hole, the tiny, ocean-bound, par-three number seven.

Nicklaus's play on the seventh was a prime example of good strategy. With the wind blowing the flag so hard that it pointed straight back at the teeing area, he tossed a few blades of grass in the air and laughed as they blew right back into his face. He chose a seven iron to make a shot of a mere 122 yards. Yet even with that much club, he had to hit it low, to avoid having the gale blow it back at him. The shot was good, placing the ball about twenty feet from the hole. He was lucky to have an uphill putt, so he rapped it firmly and seemed to breathe a sigh of relief as it went in.

As he walked to the next tee Nicklaus looked more confident. He didn't know that he had put four shots between himself and Palmer. But he was sure that conditions were bedeviling everyone in the field, and that not one of them was better prepared than he. Though Jack Nicklaus wasn't the kind to talk about God or fate and golf, he agreed with one of the philosophical points in Trevino's Sunday sermon: the importance of accepting the inevitable bad shot. He got a chance to prove it on the tenth hole.

Plotted in the Scottish style, the Pebble Beach course does not bring players back to the clubhouse at the end of the front nine holes. (The course is not meant for those committed to half a round.) Instead, from the fourth hole on, players are drawn farther and farther away from the lodge. From number six through ten, the sea is always on a player's right, roiling beneath cliffs that range from twenty to forty feet high. In places, the surf breaks against rock. But on the par-four tenth hole, where the green is just a short walk from the village of Carmel, the entire fairway is flanked by sandy beach. Though it lies fifty feet or more beneath the bluff, paths lead down to the strand, which is actually in play as a lateral hazard.

The best angle to the tenth green is on the right side of

the fairway, which means that the best drive involves the risk of landing on the beach. If he had known that the first dozen players to attack the hole had suffered bogey or worse, Nicklaus might have played more conservatively. But he didn't know this. And besides, when he missed, Nicklaus went to the left, not to the right. In the sixty-three holes he had played so far, he hadn't hit one drive to the right. He took the risk and lost when a gust of wind pushed him off balance, forcing a slice worthy of a Sunday-afternoon duffer. Suddenly Nicklaus had to decide whether or not to visit Carmel Beach.

Atop the bluff, Nicklaus stood peering over the edge like a tourist on the observation deck of the Empire State Building. The report from people on the beach below was not encouraging. The ball was buried in the sand. Just moving it would require enormous skill and strength. Lofting it up onto the fairway might be impossible, and even if he could do it, Nicklaus would still lie two and be hitting his third shot.

In the end, the decision to accept a one-stroke penalty and drop a new ball at the point where the first one flew over the cliff was easy. If he had chosen to play from the beach, and failed, he could have made a very high score on the hole. The championship, the entire Grand Slam, could be lost right there. Compared with this possibility, the medicine of a single penalty stroke hardly seemed bitter at all.

After it was dropped, the new ball sat in sandy soil at the edge of the cliff. According to Nicklaus's calculation, based on his own measured footsteps, he was 221 yards from the hole. A nice two iron, he thought, followed by two putts, and he would escape with just a scratch. He braced himself well for the swing and felt solid as the club struck the ball. And then he watched the white speck drift farther and farther to the right until it, too, disappeared over the bluff.

This time Nicklaus's ball didn't make it all the way down to the beach, and he was able to pitch it to within eight feet of the hole. Trevino waited on the green, his own ball just a little closer to the cup. Nicklaus wrestled the ball in with two putts and left with a six, his first double bogey of the entire tournament. Trevino missed his par putt, and the chance to make up two shots on the leader. From this moment on he seemed to be pulling for his playing partner to win while trying to finish his own round without too much embarrassment.

On the twelfth hole, a long par three, Nicklaus chose to hit a right-to-left draw that would bite into the wind coming off the ocean to his left and land in the perfect spot, about ten feet directly in front of the flagstick. The ball hit as softly as a stone hitting a concrete playground. It skidded and then began to roll, fast. It went through the green and down an embankment.

On his way to the ball Nicklaus violated his own habit of ignoring the leaderboards. He couldn't resist an anxious glance, and the news it brought him wasn't good. His debacle on ten had brought Arnold Palmer back into the match, just two strokes behind.

Playing ahead of Nicklaus and before an enthusiastic crowd, Palmer seemed more youthful than he had all year. He was certainly dressed like a younger man, in trousers with a psychedelic pattern that defied description. But more to the point was the determination in Palmer's eyes and the quickness in his step. He could feel that he had a chance to win.

Nicklaus found his ball in a tangle of rough resembling

the plastic grass in a child's Easter basket. Here again he faced a challenge from the rock-hard green. If he hit the ball too firmly or skulled it, he could easily put it over the green and into a bunker. With this in mind he chose to make a conservative pitch, which failed to clear the shorter rough.

With his ball nestled in four or five inches of grass, Nicklaus set himself up over it with a wedge in hand. Trevino sat down on his golf bag to rest his tired legs and focused his attention on his front-running playing partner. Nicklaus planned to hit the top half of the ball, just above its equator, let it pop onto the green, and then run toward the hole. He made the shot, but the green was so hard and fast the ball didn't stop until it was nearly ten feet beyond the hole.

The television broadcast of the 1972 Open was the most ambitious airing of a live golf match to date. The ABC network had cameras on fourteen holes, a record, and the viewers were treated to a drama that no one at Pebble Beach could have witnessed. This is because while Nicklaus was struggling to get into position for a bogey, Palmer was spinning an iron shot to within ten feet of the cup on the fourteenth hole.

And so, on a split screen, the national television audience could watch Nicklaus line up a bogey putt as Palmer went for birdie. If Palmer made his and Nicklaus missed, the aging King would grab a tie for the lead. For a moment, some of the years seemed to melt off Palmer's face and a few new wrinkles creased Nicklaus's as they both focused their minds. In an article published by *Sports Illustrated* two weeks later, Nicklaus explained what he thought.

"You've just made one double bogey. You're not going to make another one," he told himself.

Nicklaus made himself as comfortable as he could, and finally putted. The ball skittered toward the hole. "Get in there!" shouted Trevino. It moved slightly from right to left and then seemed to dive in. With the crowd around the green cheering, Nicklaus pursed his lips, nodded, and with a shake of his head hustled away like a boy who had lifted a candy bar from the corner store.

Up ahead on the fourteenth green, Arnold Palmer's ball lay to the left of the hole and a little above it. It was a tricky situation requiring a very soft touch and perfect aim to compensate for an apparent left-to-right break. Palmer walked all around the shot, like Minnesota Fats checking the lay of a table. He then stood over the putt, glancing over his left shoulder at the hole, then turning his head back to the ball. In his hand was a Tommy Armour putter that looked like the one he had used all week. But he had actually just traded a set of irons to obtain it from Aussie David Graham. Palmer needed it because he had been bending his own putter the night before, looking for some solution to his poor performance on the greens, and it had snapped in two.

When he was finally ready, Palmer hit his ball with just the right amount of force. But as it rolled downhill, it became clear that there was no break in the green. Palmer threw some body English into it, letting his knees buckle a bit and bending into a half squat. He threw his hands up into the air, raising the putter above his head. And as the ball rolled past the hole, missing by an inch, he looked away, over his right shoulder. His face was filled with pain, disbelief, and, perhaps, the realization that he might never again get this close to a Major victory.

Just as Bobby Jones was right about winners and losers at the U.S. Open, Jack Nicklaus would turn out to be right about the conditions at Pebble Beach that day. He was certain that everyone would make mistakes on the course, and they did. After his bid for the lead failed, Palmer bogeyed the next two holes. He was out of it.

Though some might say that Nicklaus backed into the Open victory, the shot he hit from the tee on the par-three seventeenth hole demolished this argument. He chose a one iron, a club so difficult to hit straight that most pros didn't carry one, and most manufacturers did not include them in sets. On that day, Nicklaus felt so confident that he could have hit the ball with a hoe, if that was all there was at hand.

"I took it [the club] back inside," he later explained. "I felt myself shut the club, and I opened it. My timing was that good."

The ball left the tee box like a cannon shot, sailed with a slight right-to-left draw, cleared a bunker in front of the green, landed five feet from the hole, bounced once, and hit the flagstick. It came to rest mere inches from the cup. With the tap-in birdie, Nicklaus had such a big lead that he could afford to three-putt the last hole and still win by three.

Coming up to the eighteenth fairway, Nicklaus learned that Bruce Crampton had made fewer mistakes than his other pursuers and sneaked into second place. (Palmer was third, while Trevino finished a respectable fourth.) When Nicklaus got to the green, Crampton smiled and held up five fingers to indicate he was five strokes over par. Nicklaus could six-putt and still win. As it was, he needed three strokes to get it in the hole.

A bogey by the champion was a fitting end to a tournament where no one would break par for the four days. Indeed, Nicklaus's score of two-over-par 290 was the second highest U.S. Open total posted since World War II. But under the conditions, he had completed a strong performance, and it brought him to the halfway mark in his Grand Slam tour, noted in the gallery.

"The Slam, Jack!" hollered one man. "You're on your way to the Slam."

Few noted that as he grasped his thirteenth Major title, Nicklaus had already equaled Bobby Jones's lifetime collection of these trophies. It had taken him a bit longer than Jones—thirteen years compared with eight—but Nicklaus had done it on longer, some would say more difficult, courses, and against fields that were much deeper in talent. Fewer still noticed that, given his PGA of America win the year before, Nicklaus held three of the four Major titles.

In the hubbub of his pressroom appearance after the victory, Nicklaus said he believed the odds of him making the sweep were down to fifty to one. Then he was interrupted for a phone call. It was President Nixon, who congratulated Nicklaus on performing well when "the chips were down." Nixon had awakened that morning to a report in the *Washington Post* about Republican Party operatives caught during a break-in at a hotel/office complex called the Watergate. America was about to plunge into the worst presidential crisis of the century.

CHAPTER 6

From now own, he's going to have
trouble even breathing.
–Arnold Palmer, on Jack Nicklaus
after his 1972 U.S. Open victory

Half a world away from Pebble Beach, California, Bruce Crampton's mother sat at a table, scissors in hand, and carefully carved the sports page of the *Sydney Herald*. The screaming headline on the first article she clipped was two inches tall and read:

NO. 2!
JACK NICKLAUS CARRIES OFF THE U.S.
OPEN AND HEADS FOR HISTORY

It was a testament to the sporting world's obsession with Nicklaus's quest that in Australia, Crampton's hometown newspaper was delirious over an American reaching the midpoint in the Grand Slam. Almost overlooked by the editors was the fact that their boy Crampton, who had quietly finished second in the Masters, had done it again at the U.S. Open. But for Nicklaus, it would have been his face in all the photographs, his name in giant type.

Such was the fate of a generation of A-level touring pros forced to compete in an era that was dominated by the kind of A-plus golfer who appears once every few decades. They are reduced to being supporting players, witnesses to the creation of a legend. As a foreigner from modest beginnings—his father was a policeman—Crampton was an astute observer of Nicklaus, America, and the PGA Tour circa 1972. He understood the jealousies other players felt, but also felt a certain privilege at being so close to history.

"One of the things that really struck me about Jack, and really about a lot of people in the States, was the scope of their ambitions," recalled Crampton. "Jack didn't want to just win tournaments, or be one of the best. His goal was to be *the* best, and not just the best of his group, but the best player *of all time*. He had really big dreams, and you know, that's where it all starts, with the idea that you can accomplish something big. You didn't see that so much in Australia in my day."

As the product of a family and a culture that discouraged showy displays and overweening ambition, Crampton nursed smaller dreams. But even with his feet on the ground, he would win fourteen titles on the regular tour and twenty on the Senior PGA Tour. For all this success, he couldn't hope to earn what a Nicklaus made in endorsements, but he accepted this fate, understanding that the galleries and purses he enjoyed every week were double what they would have been without Nicklaus in the mix. And there were moments when Nicklaus could be even more directly generous.

Crampton would always remember a frustrating session on the practice tee before the 1965 Crosby Pro–Am. He had been playing so poorly that he was thinking of withdrawing. Though his wife had persuaded him to make one last attempt at self-correction, it wasn't going well. Nothing he tried on the tee made things better until Nicklaus wandered by and offered a comment.

"Bruce, if you take the club back any more inside than you are doing right now, you're going to hit your right ankle."

He was right. Crampton had become sloppy in his take-away and was failing to get the club into position to strike the ball squarely. With Nicklaus's insight and a few dozen practice shots, he was able to recover his old dependable swing. He went on to win the tournament, and two more, in the year.

In the 1972 season, Crampton took significant abuse in the press for being overly serious and overly cautious. He was criticized for choosing to avoid the British Open. And he was portrayed as a sort of "anti-Trevino," a cold, almost unfeeling, man. The truth was much more complicated than the press and public knew. For one thing, and this would surface only after he retired, Crampton suffered from periodic bouts of clinical depression. It was a family trait, a curse that led his father and two uncles to suicide. As for the British Open, well, Crampton had his reasons.

It all began in 1957 when Crampton, then age twenty-one, won the Australian Open. He received automatic invitations to play in the 1958 Masters, and then to compete in Great Britain. It would be his first big trip abroad. In America he was dumbfounded by the praise and coddling he received in Augusta. He had never seen golfers treated so well, and he liked it.

After being courted like a prince at the Masters, Crampton crossed the Atlantic to play a series of tournaments ending with the British Open. In Scotland he was met by tournament organizers who regarded pro golfers as somewhat less respectable than hunting dogs. After enduring many inconveniences and meals unworthy of the Russian Army, he expressed his opinions in a newspaper article published in Australia but wired back to Scotland. The next day the British tabloids made him front-page news. He was disrespectful, they charged, the baddest boy in golf.

For weeks, no matter where he went, Crampton was hounded by photographers. His miserable adventure ended with the Open at Royal Lythum and St. Annes. He failed to break 80 in his first round, and then endured the abuse of a functionary who demanded he perform a sort of ritual for checking and then signing his scoreboard. (It involved being seated at a special table and then ceremoniously marching to officials across the room.) The next day Crampton missed the cut, and for the rest of his life, he felt no great attraction to golf as it was played in the land of its birth.

As he considered his friend Nicklaus's Grand Slam tour, Crampton believed that Scotland would present the biggest obstacle. It wouldn't be a matter of resentments and misunderstandings, but rather a problem with playing conditions, he thought. So much in golf as it's played in the Isles is beyond one's control. Take the allotment of tee times. If you begin play in sunny, calm weather you are blessed. A few hours later wind and rain are likely to appear, and if your tee time coincides, you are unlucky indeed.

Luck was also built into the landscape on Scottish courses. The linksland is so varied—all hills, potholes, and swales—that bad lies of the sort rarely seen on American courses are routine. The greens are so hard that it's often better to land a shot thirty yards short and let it run up onto the putting surface and roll to a stop. (This is easier when you've played the course a thousand times and know, or even feel, the land's contours.) Finally, the view a player gets on such courses—unbroken by trees and sharp landmarks—can be so subtle that yardage charts and even one's eyes can seem to be lying. Altogether, the British game is a different kind of golf, subject to the fates and the weather in ways that Crampton and other veterans of the American tour can find discomfiting.

Jack Nicklaus could do nothing about the Scottish weather, but he could prepare himself to cope with the stress that greeted him halfway to the Grand Slam. When the U.S. Open was over, he dashed from San Francisco to Great Harbor Cay in the Bahamas for a secluded family vacation, stopping only long enough at home in Florida to watch his son play a baseball game and to pick up the British golf equipment—clubs and balls—that he would use in Scotland. He planned to play a few rounds in the Bahamas to get the feel for the tools he would use in the next Major.

Weighted, balanced, and lofted to mirror his American set, Nicklaus's English-made clubs did not require he make any significant adjustments in his swing. The British ball was a different matter. A bit smaller in diameter than the American ball, it seemed to bore through the wind better. It also flew farther. Like the USGA, the ruling authorities of the British game placed no restrictions on the ball's materials. If manufacturers found a resin, a plastic, or a rubber that made it go farther, they were allowed to use it.

Most American touring pros didn't have the time to practice with the British ball and generally preferred the better spinning properties of their own. Under the rules of the Open, they would be allowed to use it. But Nicklaus had the time to make the adjustment and take advantage of the little sphere's superior stability in the wind. By the time he departed the Bahamas, he felt comfortable with the equipment. He was also beginning to let the enormity of his accomplishments to date—winning the thirteenth Major to match the Jones record—sink into his psyche. In a brief article he published in *Sports Illustrated*, he revealed just a touch of ambivalence about equaling his hero.

". . . I'm so dumbfounded, I don't know what to say," he wrote. "I look at myself and I say, 'Am I that good? Do I deserve to be there?' " As ever, history and his hero were on his mind. "I knew Bobby Jones well," wrote Nicklaus. "I like to think he would be very happy about it."

At the start of his drive for the Slam, Nicklaus had facetiously set his own odds for success at one million to one. After the Masters the figure went down to one thousand to one. When the U.S. Open title was in hand, he told the press that odds on the sweep were down to "fifty to one, a hundred to one, you name it."

For six months Nicklaus had publicly calculated his

chances in each of the Majors. When he turned to the matter of the British Open, he talked about how much he loved the tradition and challenge of the game as it is played on its native soil. As a man with his eye on history, it was natural for Nicklaus to develop this strong attachment, and he could talk about the courses and the figures of the past—Old and Young Tom Morris, Alister Mackenzie, Willie Park—with the familiarity of a native Scotsman.

The 1972 British Open venue, Muirfield, was Nicklaus's favorite among the grand old courses. Unlike so many other British courses—St. Andrews, in particular—Muirfield does not torture players with hidden hazards or blind shots. However, it is a demanding course, with huge deep bunkers in dangerous locations and fairways that narrow down to fifteen yards at certain places. Altogether it is a demanding but entirely fair test.

Nicklaus won his first British Open at Muirfield in 1966 (his second Open victory came at St. Andrews in 1970), but his affection for the place had bloomed in 1959 when he was just nineteen years old. Nicklaus had gone to Scotland to play in the Walker Cup, the biennial amateur contest of teams from America and Great Britain. He won both his matches on the Muirfield course, which he found to be fascinating and difficult. The experience led him to think even more seriously about his place in the game and its centuries-long tradition.

In 1972 the Muirfield connection made Nicklaus and many others optimistic about his capturing the third Grand Slam title. But on the same day that Nicklaus noted the improving odds, Arnold Palmer played the realist. Just as he had predicted that Lee Trevino would have trouble coping with success, Palmer said that in light of his two Major victories so far, Nicklaus's chances in Britain were reduced. Palmer reasoned that it's much harder to win three times than it is to win just once. He should have known. In 1960 he had gone to St. Andrews with the Masters and U.S. Open trophies in hand only to lose the British Open by a single stroke.

In July 1972, interest in Nicklaus was so great that the *New York Times Magazine* commissioned British historian Alistair Cooke to write an essay that all but canonized him. Cooke attributed his subject's success to his mind, not his body. "The overriding supremacy of Nicklaus," he wrote, "is due to what you might call calculated gall or generalship under pressure." In language as grandiose as the cause Nicklaus pursued, he described the test that awaited him at Muirfield as "a truly Gaelic torture."

With Cooke weighing in, it seemed that in the time between the U.S. Open and the British Open just about everyone who was concerned about the game of golf had Nicklaus on his mind. *Golf World*, the insider's weekly bible, all but declared the Slam clinched, noting, "Should a player stop Nicklaus on his seemingly impossible mission, a villain will be born." Perhaps the only voice that was silent on the subject belonged to the man who was usually most likely to say almost anything to anyone at any time—Lee Trevino.

As Nicklaus headed for beautiful Great Harbor Cay and all the ink-stained experts took to their typewriters, Lee Trevino vanished from the public arena. His agent turned down interview requests from reporters. No one answered the telephone, or the door at his El Paso home. The loudest and most visible man in golf simply disappeared.

Without telling friends or his pals on the tour, Trevino had packed his family and his clubs and driven to the one place in America he believed would offer him privacy and golfing conditions that approximated the windy Scottish coast and the wide-open, rolling fairways of Muirfield. He went, of course, to Killeen, Texas, where the pro at the new municipal course was an old Navy buddy.

If the scrubland between Austin and Waco doesn't remind you of Scotland, then you have never stood at the back door of the little clubhouse at the Killeen Municipal Golf Course. If you cover your ears to block out the scrape of cowboy boots on the concrete patio, and focus on the windblown flags and the rolling terrain, you can begin to sense the similarities. Almost every shot that lands on the fairways at Killeen finds a hillside lie. The ground is dry, hard, and fast. The greens are, too. The rough grows like Scottish heather in places, and on every hole you've got to contend with the wind. Sometimes it blows in two different directions at once.

If you want to be picky about it, then you can find some aspects of summer golf in central Texas that diverge from the conditions in Great Britain. For one thing, it's a lot hotter. For another, there is the absence of mature, truly knowledgeable caddies. But the ever resourceful Trevino found a way around these problems.

Each morning that he awoke in a little house he borrowed from Orville Moody, Trevino rushed to get to the golf course before the sun. While the birds were beginning to cackle and chirp, he strapped his golf bag onto the back of a motorized cart and smiled at the young girl—a daughter of the club superintendent—whom he was paying to drive. In the cool of the dawn he would tee off and then start running toward his ball, with the girl in pursuit. For eighteen holes he would practice keeping the ball low off the tee and bouncing it onto the greens. And he would run the entire course to rebuild the stamina and strength he might have lost in the hospital before the U.S. Open.

Since his helper was deaf, and Trevino didn't know sign language, they raced around together in silence. This made it easy for Trevino to keep his entire focus on his game. A hand signal would keep his bag and clubs present when he decided to drop another ball and try a shot a second time. Another wave of the hand and the two were off, like a fox and a hound.

The morning practice would end at about the time that flight crews began warming up the planes at a military airfield that ran alongside the Killeen course. Trevino would clean up, eat breakfast, and then spend the middle part of the day with his family. They often took picnics to the banks of a nearby river. At about 4 P.M. he would go back to work, hitting hundreds of balls on the driving range, or playing another round, and imagining a victory in Scotland.

For Trevino, the British Open at Muirfield presented a rare combination of challenge and opportunity. As returning champion, he was eager to defend his title. Back-to-back Open victories were precious. Palmer had done it in 1961 and 1962. Prior to that it was Peter Thomson, who won three times, from 1954 to 1956. But that was before the Open became a true modern Major, attracting all the best American players.

Since then only Palmer had defended and won. The list of those champions who failed to repeat included Player, Nicklaus (twice), and Tony Jacklin.

Beyond the challenge of defending his title at Muirfield, Trevino and every other man in the field had their best opportunity to stop Nicklaus before he achieved the Slam. Once he returned to America, where the PGA Championship would be played at Oakland Hills, outside Detroit, Nicklaus's length and mastery of "target" golf gave him too many advantages. In contrast, Muirfield demanded accuracy and intelligence more than power. The Scottish weather, which often had a sort of leveling effect on the contestants, also made an upset more likely.

For all the reasons Trevino might cite as motivation, one additional factor weighed heavily in his favor—his love affair with golf in Great Britain. Beginning with his first visit in 1969, when he discovered that many British courses were "like Tenison Park without trees," Lee Trevino had been as mad about England as the most rabid Beatles fan. In fact, during his Open victory the year before, Trevino was overheard mangling Beatles tunes as he ad-libbed his way from one hole to the next.

Trevino's response to British culture was the opposite of Crampton's, and it had made him a hero of the working class. He was always doing something that got him positive coverage in the papers. Informed that he needed to acquire a suit and tie to reside at the Savoy Hotel, he rented a tuxedo, top hat, cape, and cane. The photos of him dressed so formally appeared in most of the nation's newspapers with comic captions. On the golf course Trevino was flabbergasted by the funereal silence of the galleries. He made a point of engaging with the crowds, and soon they were talking back.

Though his clowning won over many fans, the rest were charmed by Trevino's praise for their country's courses. He genuinely appreciated the respect that greenkeepers demonstrated when they donned coat and tie before starting their mowers. He was thrilled to play before so many people who understood the game, and its nuances, well enough to applaud the best shots and recognize lucky mistakes for what they were.

On the final day of the 1971 British Open, Trevino had faced a challenge from Lu Liang Huan of Taiwan. The two had met years before when Trevino, a Marine, was based in the Pacific. Lu gave Trevino a playful nickname—Bird—in honor of the way his drives flew, then trounced him in match play. At Royal Birkdale they greeted each other like old friends. As they teed off, Trevino was one shot ahead, and over the first nine holes he increased his lead by four shots. The gallery got behind Trevino as he threw his body into every shot, even collapsing onto his knees when a very long putt rolled into the cup.

After making the turn with a huge advantage, Trevino allowed the match to become more exciting than it should have been. He followed two bogeys with a double on the seventeenth hole. On the 500-yard number eighteen, he hit a huge drive and a long six iron to reach the green in two. Meanwhile, with his own second shot, Lu somehow managed to strike a woman in the gallery. She was briefly unconscious, but awoke and wished Lu good luck. He made a putt for birdie, but so did Trevino, winning by the same margin he held on the first tee.

If his raucous performance on the course hadn't been enough to win over the British fans, Trevino sealed his relationship that night. He promised to donate $5,000 from his winnings to a local orphanage, but only if the nuns who ran it joined him for champagne. They did. He wrote the check, and then raffled off his golf clubs with the proceeds going to the nuns as well.

Though many casual observers would assume that the more erudite Nicklaus, with his passion for history and classical swing, was the American player most suited to the British Open, Trevino would always disagree. He knew he was the favorite of fish-and-vinegar crowds, who agreed that his scrappy, creative style was a better fit. "If I had played over there from the age of twenty, like Jack, I would have won it five or six times," said Trevino. "I really loved it over there."

With Trevino, Nicklaus, Palmer, and Player all practicing for the upcoming Major "over there," they made room at the top of PGA Tour scoreboards for a host of players who relished the opportunity to compete without the superstars present. Jim Jamieson, who had delighted the gallery at the Masters with his department-store putter, took full advantage in the week following the U.S. Open at the Western Open in Chicago.

Cheered on by a crowd from his hometown of Moline, Jamieson charged into the tournament with three birdies and an eagle on the first five holes. With scores of 68, 67, and 67, he took an eight-shot lead into the final day. (This was the widest Sunday morning advantage posted at any tournament all year.) He ended up winning by six, capturing his first victory in four years on tour, and netting $30,000.

Jamieson, who seemed to be a crowd favorite everywhere he played, was met on the eighteenth green by a cheering section made up of his fellow pros. He celebrated with a few hundred "friends" and carried his baby son Jay around in the huge trophy cup.

For Jamieson, the Western Open win may have meant more than the Slam meant to Nicklaus. Nicklaus's fortune and future in golf were secure. He would be welcomed to play anywhere in the world for as long as he could swing a club. In contrast, because of his low earnings, Jamieson had come close to losing his playing privileges several times in his short career. He had sponsors to repay (including the founder of the Dairy Queen chain), and no big endorsement contracts to supply cash for the times when he didn't make the cut. Winning meant that he could stop wondering and worrying, at least for a year.

The week after the Western Open, with the big four still absent, David Graham, whose main achievement at Pebble Beach had come in trading Arnold Palmer a putter, won the Cleveland Open and its $30,000 prize. Using the irons he had gotten from Palmer, Graham won the title by beating his friend Bruce Devlin in a play-off. Like Jamieson, Graham was a first-time winner. It had taken him three years.

Cleveland was good to a number of other players. On Sunday, Buddy Allin was just three shots off the lead, and he finished in seventh place, earning more than $4,000 in prize money. The cash allowed him to move back into the top sixty on the money list. If he could stay there he would have full playing privileges for the next season. Another player who benefited with the premier players nowhere in sight was rookie Lanny Wadkins, who came in fourth.

The reprieve from superstar competition ended the next week, as Palmer and Player joined defending champion Trevino for the Canadian Open in Fort Erie, Ontario. While Nicklaus had gone early to Muirfield, the other three paid their respects to the Canadian fans and golf establishment and used the competitive setting as their final pre-Major tune-up. Though he put up a creditable defense, Trevino lost the title to veteran Gay Brewer, who took the lead on the first day and never lost it. (In winning, Brewer ended a five-year victory drought and earned a spot in the upcoming World Series of golf. This televised event, with a $50,000 first prize, usually featured the victors from the British and American Opens along with the winners of the PGA Championship and the Masters. When one man captured two of these titles, the Canadian Open victor was added to the field.) Palmer and Player also performed well at Fort Erie. Each finished under par, showing they were ready for Scotland.

The moment they putted-out on the final hole of the Canadian tournament, Palmer, Player, and Trevino each dashed to the airport to begin their long journeys across the Atlantic. Trevino and Player would fly from Toronto. Palmer would pilot his own plane home to Latrobe, Pennsylvania, to pick up his wife, Winnie, then skip over to New York for the last transatlantic flight to leave Kennedy Airport that night.

Palmer, Player, and Trevino would join a host of America's best golfers, each of whom were intent upon stopping the Nicklaus Slam. Among them were Tom Weiskopf, who beat Nicklaus in Fort Lauderdale; Johnny Miller, the rising star; Jerry Heard, now third on the U.S. money list; and Doug Sanders. For the Scots, Sanders would always be a sentimental favorite. In 1970 he had come to the eighteenth hole at St. Andrews needing a par to beat Nicklaus by one and take his first Major. He had reached this moment by hitting one of the greatest shots ever seen at St. Andrews. It had come on the seventeenth when he managed to get out of one of the course's dreaded pot bunkers and send his ball to within inches of the hole.

On the finishing hole of that fated round, Sanders hit a solid drive to within one hundred yards of the green. But then he abandoned the style of play that had gotten him this far—the Scottish bump and run—and chose to try an American-style high wedge shot to the green. As most in the gallery would have expected, the ball didn't hold, but instead ran thirty-five feet past the cup. Sanders then made a decent lag putt to within four feet.

Though it was a short distance, the four-foot putt Sanders needed to win was not easy. It was a downhiller, with a left-to-right break that was almost impossible to see. Sanders didn't. He missed. Nicklaus would tie him, and then beat him in a play-off. (He came to call Sanders's missed putt "one of the luckiest breaks of my career.") But while Nicklaus got the trophy, Sanders won the hearts of many Scots who, thirty years later, would still call a heartbreaking miss "a Sanders-poot."

As he traveled to Great Britain, Doug Sanders anticipated finding a certain splendid isolation in the landscape. Windswept Scottish courses always seemed to make him feel more relaxed, more confident, alone with the game. In such an ancient place, where golf was cherished, even revered, Sanders felt like every course was his home course.

CHAPTER 7

I don't think golf was ever intended to be fair.
—Jack Nicklaus, prior to the
1972 British Open

The first round of the 1972 British Open was a full week away, and yet Jack Nicklaus was already cozied into Greywalls, a twenty-two-room hotel made of honey-colored stone that overlooks the Muirfield course. Few places could fulfill an American's fantasy of Scotland better than Muirfield and Greywalls. Twenty miles west of the city of Edinburgh, Muirfield is a seaside moor—there's no town or village called Muirfield—that runs along the Firth of Forth in a region of castles, fishing villages, manors, and farms called East Lothian. The hotel, with its paneled library, rose garden, and holly hedges, is the kind of place that quiets the mind and fills the heart with Shakespearean fantasy.

Even in summer, visitors at Greywalls may find a fire burning as a cold wind and rain slash in off the sea. This was the weather for which Nicklaus had prepared, but he found instead the kind of warm, breezy, and slightly humid conditions common to summer days in Columbus, Ohio. He also found, in all of Great Britain, a commonwealth agog with the notion of a Nicklaus Slam.

Speculation on Nicklaus's chances for his third Major had begun as soon as the U.S. Open was finished. The *London Observer*'s golf commentator flatly predicted a Nicklaus win. Both the *Edinburgh Scotsman* and the *Manchester Guardian* decorated their pre-Open coverage with special panels featuring Nicklaus portraits. The *Scotsman* went so far as to rename the tournament the Grand Slam Open.

While sports page opinion must be considered with a generous dose of salt, oddsmakers in the legal betting shops were a more dependable and hard-hearted source of Open forecasts. They made Nicklaus the strongest favorite in the Open's 101-year history, giving him odds of just a bit over two to one. Lee Trevino, the defending champ, was next at six to one. Farther down on the tout sheets, Gary Player, who won the 1959 Open at Muirfield, was given ten to one. The odds of an Arnold Palmer victory were sixteen to one, while Tom Weiskopf was twenty to one. Tony Jacklin, the Englishman who carried all of Britain's hopes, was rated no better than Weiskopf. Of course, in the popular mind, the memory of Jacklin reclaiming the Open title for his country in 1969, after foreigners had held the title for eighteen years, was still fresh enough to make him a gallery favorite.

When it comes to both knowledge of and passion for the game, Scottish golf fans surpass even those in Augusta, Georgia. And the prideful sense that the game itself is their possession may be strongest in Edinburgh and its surrounding countryside. No place has a greater claim on golf history. Founded in 1744, the Honourable Company of Edinburgh Golfers created the first rules of the game a full ten years before the better-known Royal and Ancient Golf Club of St. Andrews was created. When the Edinburgh company lost its first and second homes, it had Old Tom Morris lay out and build the Muirfield course, which opened in 1891. Distinctly private, the club became known as a fortress of tradition and the site of many historic tournaments won by the likes of Vardon, Hagen, and yes, Nicklaus.

All of Muirfield's history, combined with the dramatic rolling seaside landscape, could make a visitor feel awestruck and small. "The place produces a certain feeling of unworthiness in the average player," noted golf course architect Desmond Muirhead. Members at Muirfield were so committed to the purity of the game that they never saw the need for a club pro. And touring professionals were treated like third-class citizens, added Muirhead, "until the Prince of Wales brought Walter Hagen in the front door in 1929."

By 1972, Nicklaus could enter the clubhouse without the aid of a prince, but he still had to figure out the golf course. He gave himself a full week to settle on some overarching principles for playing on the moor and to devise specific bits of strategy for each hole.

At less than 6,900 yards, Muirfield was not a particularly long course, but the wind could make it play much longer. Players are challenged to place their drives where a comfortable second shot might be made. This meant that every tee shot required careful thought about what would follow. Sometimes choosing to hit a shorter drive, with an iron or three wood, would be the best play.

The second major concern at Muirfield involved the hard, fast greens. Many newcomers assumed that the best way to get the ball on and keep it on was to land a low shot in front of the green and let it roll to a stop. But this kind of bump-and-run shot was perilous, because as the ball scooted to the green it could be diverted by any hillock, rabbit hole, or tuft of grass it met. Obviously, the player who understood the land and the weather and chose the right technique, at the right time, would have a distinct advantage.

Beyond these two general themes, each of the holes at Muirfield demanded a well-considered strategy. Gary Player and many others considered Muirfield's par-four first the toughest starting hole in the world. It required an accurate drive—usually into the prevailing wind—to a spot less than twenty yards in width. (The best place to land was toward the left, but a dangerous bunker lurked there.) Beyond lay a green heavily guarded by sand bunkers, where it was easy to waste two strokes to get out. At the 1966 Open at Muirfield, most players made bogey or worse on the first hole. Italian Dino Canonica scored a nine there to start one of his rounds.

The other particularly difficult holes at Muirfield included number nine, where a ridge in the fairway fed drives into a series of bunkers and the second shot was threatened by a long gray wall noting out of bounds along the left side. Two near-perfect shots were needed to par the eighteenth hole, which rose to a slick green that at Open time was flanked by temporary grandstands that could hold 7,000 people. When he won the Open at Muirfield in 1959, Gary Player finished with a double bogey on this hole after driving into one of the three bunkers on the left side of the fairway.

As he practiced on the course in July 1972, Jack Nicklaus concluded that the number one tee shot would be the most difficult shot in every round. Assuming that the wind would blow, and the pressure would be intense, he decided on a conservative approach. He would use a long iron on the first hole and on other tees, and hit few woods from the tees. (In 1966 he had used his driver only seventeen times in four complete rounds.) Nicklaus decided that he would target safe areas on the greens, not the flagsticks. And most of all, he would try to stay out of the rough and out of the bunkers.

On the weekend before the tournament began, while most of the PGA Tour was at the Canadian Open, Nicklaus was joined at Greywalls by his friend Tom Weiskopf. They played on Saturday in a group that also included Tony Jacklin and Hugh Jackson. With the sun burning hot and the wind becalmed, Weiskopf shot a 64—including seven birdies and an eagle—which equaled the record for the course. Nicklaus would use his friend's performance to divert some of the press's attention. Watch out for this man once the Open starts, he said. But Weiskopf would have none of it. He understood that a terrific score that can't be posted on a tournament card meant little. However, he could accept that in general, his game was getting a little better.

"I could see my game developing at that time, getting closer to the level where winning a Major was possible," recalled Weiskopf, years later. "I was learning how to gear up for those four events that give you a chance to be part of history. At most of them, because of the pressure, there are really only about ten guys who have a real chance. I liked to think I was one of those ten, but obviously Jack was the one that everyone expected to be there at the end."

Weiskopf was learning from Nicklaus how to bring his game to a peak as the Major tournaments began. At Muirfield this meant enjoying a full week to adjust his body to the stressful change in time zones caused by air travel. By Monday morning, when a well-rested Nicklaus awoke at Greywalls, many of his challengers were stumbling off jetliners that had crossed the Atlantic overnight. Each would follow his own strategy for adaptation. The most common involved simply staying awake until the evening, when exhaustion became irresistible. Gary Player, ever conscious of his health, clearly regretted that he had so little time to adjust. "Arriving this late is a bit stupid," he fumed, "not the way to set about stopping Nicklaus."

Most of the Americans came to Scotland through Prestwick International Airport, which is west of Glasgow, and then took a domestic airline flight to the smaller airport near Edinburgh. One exception was Arnold Palmer, who had a private plane waiting at Prestwick to deliver him to a country airstrip almost within sight of the golf course. By noon he was on the first tee, with his caddie Tip Anderson helping more than usual with distances, because his boss had decided to forgo both glasses and contact lenses for the week. Palmer was game, but he had quietly concluded that his prospects were slim.

Though they didn't enjoy private plane rides, almost all

of the other incoming Yanks were met at Edinburgh by drivers who were hired by the tournament to safely and swiftly bring them across Scotland. The exception was the defending champion. Early Monday morning, Lee Trevino, his wife, Claudia, and a half dozen friends made the mistake of getting off their plane in Prestwick without realizing they needed to make a connection. They trundled through the customs hall and out onto the sidewalk to discover they were alone. No car. No driver. No committeeman from the Open. Not even Trevino's loyal caddie, Willie Aitchison. Calls were made. Open officials said that yes, cars *were* waiting for them, at *Edinburgh.*

After some confusion, Trevino and company hired a van and driver, packed their dozens of suitcases and golf bags in the vehicle, and took off for what became a half-day adventure in the countryside. "We were looking for this place called Gifford, and the house we had rented—Yesterhouse," recalled Trevino. "After we drove around a lot we stopped to ask this farmer on a tractor. He says 'You canna' miss it' and tells us take this left, go twelve miles, take that right. Well, we drive and drive, doing what he says, and still can't find it. Finally we see a farmer on the other side of the road and we stop and ask him. It's the same guy. We'd gone in a goddamn circle!"

Trevino finally found Yesterhouse, dropped off his weary entourage, and then went to the golf course in the late afternoon, finding it jammed with a record number of practice-day spectators. The famous wind had begun to blow, and rain showers were moving through the area. Determined to stay awake until nighttime and force his body to adjust quickly to the time change, Trevino laced on his spikes and went looking for a game.

As he walked onto the course Trevino almost stumbled over Lu Liang Huan–"Birrrrd!"–and immediately arranged to play a round with the first group he met, which included Norman Wood and Sam Torrance. Thanks to the long daylight hours of Scottish summer, they were able to play a full eighteen holes. Trevino experimented with both balls, using the British one for long holes and the American one on the downwind par threes, where he made two pars and a birdie.

Because the British Open is moved among a rota of courses, it was the first time Trevino had ever seen Muirfield, but he quickly settled on a strategy for approaching the hard, fast greens. Where running the ball up seemed dangerous, he would hit his natural left-to-right fade a bit higher than usual, and pray for soft landings.

Prayer was very much on Trevino's mind as he said that the best a player could do to prepare for Muirfield was to "go to church." Of course he didn't have much time for church or chapel because his local sponsors, including the manufacturer of Sombrero golf clubs, put him on a busy schedule of banquet appearances and factory tours. Trevino's win the year prior, and his generosity with nuns and orphans, had made him more popular than he wanted to be. But even as he worried aloud about how he should be at Muirfield getting to know the old course, he smiled and joked with workers in overalls. It was the price of being a blue-collar hero.

Like many of the other Americans, Trevino's adjustment to this slightly foreign land included a somewhat funny turn toward Briticisms in his speech. "I don't fancy my chance as much as last year," he was heard to say. Formality didn't dampen his sense of humor, though. When he heard that his first-round playing partner was upset because the defending champ would attract a large, distracting gallery, Trevino quipped, "They're *his* people. There ain't a Mexican in the bunch."

Jack Nicklaus thought that Muirfield, in its hard, dry condition, was tougher than the Pebble Beach course he had played a month earlier. The greens were even more difficult to hold, and the racy fairways tended to shuttle balls into the bunkers and knee-high rough. Add some brisk winds, and the entire field would feel the pressure. At least he hoped they would. Nicklaus believed that he handled adversity better than anyone. The more the wind blew, he thought, the better his chances of sailing away with the trophy called the Claret Jug.

But there was only a mild breeze blowing on Wednesday morning for the start of the championship. The warm air that had dominated Scotland's weather the previous week returned, bringing heavy clouds that would produce light afternoon showers. Umbrellas snapped open in the gallery, caddies flipped up the hoods on their nylon jackets, and play continued.

Nicklaus, who appeared in a striking royal blue sweater and matching turtleneck shirt, stuck with his plan. He used his driver only five times and teed off with irons on the rest of the holes in hopes of staying out of trouble. It was the same idea he had followed at Pebble Beach, and here also he ran into a little difficulty with it. His tee shots landed in the rough seven times, probably the result of a problem with his tempo. He was swinging a little too fast, pulling the ball to the left.

With each visit to the tall rough, Nicklaus's caddie Jimmy Dickinson grew a little more dour. A lean, black-haired man of middle age, Dickinson had a stony face with a jutting chin and a thin mouth set in an almost permanent frown. He had first caddied for Nicklaus at the 1963 Open, and was on the bag again when Nicklaus won the Open at Muirfield in 1966. The partnership endured.

Many Americans formed long-term relationships with their British caddies. It was calming to see a familiar face and hear a familiar voice whenever they came to play the Open. In 1960, Arnold Palmer had James "Tip" Anderson at his side when he played in, and almost won, his first Open. Their relationship would last a remarkable thirty years, until Anderson grew too old to shoulder the bag. The relationship worked for both men. Palmer got a steady mate. And Anderson played on his Palmer connection to double his fees and become famous as the best caddie in Scotland.

In 1972, considering the way Jimmy Dickinson frowned, and almost everyone else talked about Nicklaus's first-round performance, you would have thought that he had lost the struggle against par. In fact he had scored four birdies and three bogeys to finish at 70, one under. He had been well positioned to finish one stroke lower when he hit a nearly perfect one iron shot onto the eighteenth green. However, an unlucky bounce sent the ball into a bunker. One blast and two putts gave him a bogey and held him in the 70s.

He was joined there by fellow American pro Frank Beard, who had stuck with the bigger ball and equaled the lowest score of the day on the back nine, a 34. Though Beard had won tournaments and had been the top money winner in 1969, the pressure of competition—especially the pressure he applied to himself—had gotten the best of him. He came to Muirfield ranking below the top sixty on the PGA Tour money list. He did not expect to win. In fact, he believed that Nicklaus was almost destined to claim the title on his way to a complete Slam. But a good showing at the Open would restore his confidence.

"Like most of us, I knew I was never going to be as good as Palmer and Nicklaus, but my game could reach a peak where I might win if the other guys didn't peak that week, too," he would recall. "I was always looking for that experience, that week when it happened."

Just two competitors scored better than Nicklaus and Beard on Wednesday. One was British favorite Tony Jacklin, who bogeyed the tough first hole but then made a long birdie putt on three to pull even. He played more daring golf than the rest, taking advantage of the windless day to shoot straight at the pins. This produced a flurry of birdies, but also some bogeys. He finished at 69. This was more than enough to draw a huge gallery and great cheers as he holed out for a bogey on eighteen.

The Scottish fans understood that Jacklin was the only British player with the game and the style to take on the Americans. The son of a truck driver, he was both handsome and a bit cocky, driving up to the club in a gold-colored Rolls-Royce and making it clear he wasn't intimidated by anyone.

Fearlessness was not quite the attitude struck by the other son of Britain who happened to play extremely well on the first day of the Open. Twenty-two-year-old Peter Tupling had four birdies and just one bogey to finish the day alone in the lead at 68. This fortune left him looking both stunned and bemused.

"There is no way I can win this Open, much though I would like to," he blurted after signing his scorecard. "It's not on, by the law of averages, for me to string together four rounds under seventy. I'm just not that good a player, though I feel that one day I will be."

Considering the record of this skinny young man with the pale face and bushy hair, it was hard to disagree. The British boys' champion of 1967, Tupling had only been a pro for two years. In the current season he had earned less than $750 in tournament play. He was so lightly regarded even by the Scots that he and his partner, another little-known player named Hedley Muscroft, had no gallery at all until Nicklaus finished ahead of them and a few people wandered back to discover them on the incoming nine. Tupling—pronounced Tuhpling—was remarkably cool to the end of his round. He cleared the bunkers in front of the eighteenth green with a second shot that rolled to within eight feet of the hole. He barely missed the putt for a birdie that would have placed him two shots clear of everyone else. As it was, Tupling had bested 152 of the world's best golfers, including the defending champion Lee Trevino, by three or more shots.

Trevino had arrived at the first tee snapping some chewing gum and throwing out jokes to the gallery. Glancing up at the clouds, he said, "If I lived here I could get a light complexion." Seagulls wheeled and cried overhead as he slashed a drive down the first fairway and took off after it like a hound. He went out in 36 and came home in 35 for a comfortable par round.

Just like Nicklaus, Trevino had held to his game plan, using a wider stance that made his swing look stranger than usual but produced fine results. A good example of his approach came at the short, par-four second hole. He teed off with a six iron and then hit a high, soft cut shot that stayed on the green. When he had the chance, he did use his power. On the very long par-five fifth hole he drove the ball so far that he easily reached the green with his second shot, a cut four iron. He then made a two-putt birdie.

On a course where almost everyone else hit low, running shots onto the green, Trevino's approach was unusual. Nicklaus, Weiskopf, and many others didn't believe that anyone, not even the artful Trevino, could produce such soft-landing shots on a predictable basis. They expected he would rack up a great many bogeys as the hard greens refused to accept his shots.

Since the rules allowed a change on each tee, Trevino switched freely from the British ball, which he used on longer holes, to the better-spinning American model on the short ones. Despite his success, Trevino hustled to the practice range immediately after his round, insisting he needed to hit a few hundred balls to recover his "feel."

For his part, Nicklaus seemed to have trouble deciding whether he had played poorly—since he spent so much time in the rough—or well, because his score was below par. He questioned his own decision to play a lot of pitch-and-run shots, noting he was always more comfortable lofting the ball at the flagsticks. Though he never said it, some of his discomfort may have been due to the fact that for the first time all year, in nine days of play at Major tournaments, he had not finished the day in first place.

On Thursday morning, Jack Nicklaus left Greywalls for his second round well prepared for a typical day on the Scottish coast. He wore a heavy white turtleneck sweater over a shirt that he had cut the collar from to make it more comfortable. But as the morning wore on, the temperatures climbed into the seventies, and Nicklaus began to bake.

Coming into the ninth hole, Nicklaus was blessed by a little luck. After driving the ball into the rough, his recovery shot hit the stone wall along the left side of the fairway. The ball caromed off it and came to rest right in front of the green. After a chip and a putt he trotted back to Greywalls—which sits near the tenth tee—to change clothes (a white shirt and salmon-pink cardigan). He was quick enough to avoid slowing play and any penalty that might have caused.

A change of shirt didn't produce an immediate change in Nicklaus's fortunes. Though conditions were ideal for attacking—Nicklaus thought someone might shoot 65 or better—he had continued to play conservatively, aiming for greens, not pins, and scoring routine pars. (He would later reveal that a soreness in his neck, likely caused by an awkward sleeping position, also kept him from being more aggressive.) He had suffered bogeys on the sixth and seventh holes without making a single birdie. After changing clothes he made bogey on ten, but then scrambled to make three birdies on the back nine. Altogether he scored two strokes worse than he had on Wednesday.

Afterward, Nicklaus was realistic and a bit philosophical, admitting that he had assumed he would score in the 60s given the conditions. "I didn't play well at all," he said. Then he added that he must still have all of his best shots in reserve because "I haven't wasted" any of them so far.

While others complained about the placement of the holes—tournament officials had put many of them in tricky spots on the greens—Nicklaus had been bothered more by the look of the golf course. Scottish links are essentially treeless expanses of grass, flowers, and weeds colored different shades of green, brown, and sepia. On a cool, clear day it is difficult to judge distances on such a landscape. When heat produces haze, and shimmering little mirages, it becomes almost impossible. Alignment, club selection, and swing speed are all affected.

Though Nicklaus looked tense and frustrated, he never lost his patience. The mercurial Trevino did. The first breeze of the day began as Trevino, in a bright red sweater and matching leather glove, addressed his ball at an hour when much of Britain was sitting down to tea. More serious and more quiet than usual, he played quickly, especially on the greens where he rolled in his putts with a solid self-assurance. Then, coming up the seventeenth fairway, he was distracted by the blare of television sets inside a tent that had been pitched for spectator parties. He complained to officials, who had the volume on the sets turned down. (Afterward, Trevino, still a bit hot, said that if the crowd in the tent cost him a victory he would "throw gasoline on all of those tents and set fire to them.") With the televisions quiet, Trevino made his par, which gave him a 70 for the round and, in the end, a share of the lead with Tony Jacklin.

As Jacklin thrilled Scottish hearts, Doug Sanders broke them with a debacle on the eighteenth hole. Captivated by his St. Andrews tragedy a year earlier, the locals couldn't have loved Sanders more if he had been a native. A hard-drinking, hard-living man, Sanders owned hundreds of matching golf outfits and often looked as much a lounge singer as an athlete. Appearance was so important to him that he dyed his spiked golf shoes to match his trousers, and after the actor Sean Connery sent him a playful note about his underwear, he began having it dyed as well. He walked around the golf course as if it were a casino and he the highest roller. Upon his arrival at Muirfield he had declared that he would be satisfied with nothing less than the jackpot. For the first seventeen holes on Thursday, he played like a man who would get his satisfaction.

Sanders had become the leader on the fifteenth hole when he rolled in a fifty-foot putt, bowed to the crowd, and thrust his putter into an invisible scabbard as if it were a sword. He stretched his lead to two with another birdie on seventeen and walked toward the tee to thunderous applause.

Standing on the eighteenth tee, resplendent in matching apricot-colored shirt, sweater, trousers, and shoes, Sanders was three shots under par for the day, four shots under for the tournament. He pushed his drive into one of the three bunkers on the right side of the fairway, but could easily salvage par by blasting a shot out onto the fairway.

The bunker was so deep that when Sanders entered it and settled into his stance, all the spectators could see was the silver and brown hair atop his head. Refusing to play safely out into the fairway, he tried a heroic shot for the green. It went right and landed in the tall rough. As Sanders climbed out, his caddie, a young man with a Beatles-style moptop, shook his head and lit a cigarette.

A simple bogey would have kept Sanders on top. He fidgeted uncomfortably as he stood in the knee-high grass, looking at his ball. His normal swing was quick and wristy, but this time he was even more rushed. He slapped at the ball and sent it skittering across the green into a position that was far worse.

Lying three, Sanders's ball was stuck in tangled grass on the top of a gentle slope behind the green. The little hillside was canted to the right and shaped to pour a weak chip right down a little bunker. The one thing Sanders had to avoid was a shot that was too short, and of course, that's what he produced. He flubbed his shot and his shoulders slumped as the ball trickled into the danger zone and down to the bottom of the bunker.

In the gallery, Scotsmen began biting their nails and a few of the women, their heads wrapped in kerchiefs against the wind, buried their faces in their hands. The ball lay just a foot and a half into the bunker. Sanders took an awkward stance—one foot on the grass slope above the ball, the other in the sand—and pitched it past the hole. Two putts later, he was writing a seven on his scorecard.

Later, in the pressroom, Sanders delivered one of the most honest self-assessments any athlete has ever uttered anywhere.

He began by explaining that the smart play from that first bunker would have been a plain sideways pitch to the fairway.

"But *no*, I have to be the *big man* and go for it," he said.

He then recalled how he tried to finesse his chip from the back of the green, hoping to cozy the ball close to the pin while avoiding the bunker to his right.

"I cut it too fine and the ball went into the sand. That's four. I get out in five and two-putt for whatever you call it. I'm just dumb. I'm stupid."

The misfortune that the veteran Sanders suffered that Thursday on Muirfield's final hole was balanced by young Johnny Miller's extraordinary experience on the fifth. At 560 yards, number five at Muirfield is the longest but not the most difficult hole on the course. It curves gently left to right along the duneland on the north boundary of the property. It is heavily bunkered, but the fairway is more generous than others. And in the calm, fast conditions that prevailed, many players found it relatively easy to reach the green in two shots.

Miller, whose power and appearance reminded everyone of Nicklaus, came to the fifth tee in even par. He placed his drive about 300 yards out. He then asked his caddie for his three wood—a club he had swung the day before to disastrous results—and set himself. The swing was pure Miller, long, slow, graceful. The ball flew to just before the green, jumped forward, and then disappeared from view. It was only after Miller reached the spot where it landed, and heard the crowd shouting and applauding, that he understood it had rolled in the hole. A score of two on a par-five hole was either a double eagle (the American term) or an albatross (the British name). He followed it with two birdies and eleven pars to post a score of 66. It was a tournament record on this course. Joined with the 76 Miller had made the day before, it gave him second place at day's end.

Alongside Miller on the scoreboard were Tupling, Nicklaus, Sanders, and Gary Player. The South African had put together steady par rounds, and sat one shot off the lead, but was thoroughly dissatisfied. Why? Because under the conditions that existed at Muirfield on Thursday—sunshine, dead calm winds, rough of only modest depth—a par score was, he said, "atrocious." The only reason he could offer for the fact that only six of his competitors shot below par was the pressure that came with such high stakes. If the tournament were "the Memphis Open," he said, "they would be queuing up eight under par."

For the second time this season Jack Nicklaus awoke to find he was not leading the field in a Major tournament. At Greywalls, the breakfast conversation was light. The Grand Slam was definitely not discussed. But it certainly was on the minds and tongues of almost every one of the 17,101 people who trundled onto Muirfield's rolling landscape to watch the day's play. As a topic of speculation it was right up there with the hope that Jacklin would win it again for the sake of his country and its grand game.

With the weather again ideal, it was natural to expect that a good number of the competitors would finally post lower scores. They were the greatest players in the world, and Muirfield without wind was more kitten than tiger. Officials had made their task even easier by choosing pin placements that were less tricky than they had been the day before. This was done, they explained, because sun and wind had dried the greens so much that they were treacherously fast. It would be cruel to add tough hole positions to the challenge.

Though all the variables pointed to low scores, perhaps even record-setting numbers, Lee Trevino was almost positive it wouldn't happen. As he hit balls on the practice range, searching for the right tempo and feel in his swing, he believed that if a trend emerged this day it would favor higher scores, not lower ones. And they would likely be higher still come Saturday and the final round. It was the pressure, he thought. When a Major—some would call this *The Major*—is at stake, most players get too tight to play their best. Their swings get quick or sloppy. Emotion affects judgment, the way it had Thursday with Sanders on the eighteenth hole.

Confidence would be even more important than usual, and here Trevino had an advantage. He truly believed that his hard work would be rewarded according to some divine plan. With his workouts in Killeen, his play at the Canadian Open, and his wearying trip across the Atlantic, he knew he had put in maximum effort to get this far. He felt deserving of a victory, and this made him feel like he could make any shot required to achieve it.

Trevino and Jacklin were paired in the final Friday group, teeing off at 3:33 P.M. Gary Player and Jack Nicklaus were fifteen minutes ahead. Farther ahead were Sanders and Tupling. As they played on in the endless Scottish afternoon, the Mexican American and the Englishman could see on the scoreboards the pace being set by the chief competitors. Nicklaus began with a bogey on number one—that most difficult of starting holes—and didn't make up for it until the ninth, a relatively short par five, where his power gave him an easy birdie. On the back nine, his bogeys on twelve and fourteen signaled that he wasn't going to break open the contest.

Alongside Nicklaus, Gary Player lumbered to a disorganized score of 76. His performance on the eighth hole was typical. Hoping to take a shortcut to the green, he played his drive into the practice area on the right of the tee. However, his second shot fell short—he likely chose the wrong club—and he had to struggle just for a bogey. Trevino's pressure-equals-bogeys theory was holding true.

Uncharacteristically grim-faced, Doug Sanders was dressed all in white, as if ready for Wimbledon. On the ninth he pitched his third shot from alongside the gray stone wall and then rolled in a long birdie putt to seize the lead. But he was undone on the fourteenth. The snap and click of a photographer's camera disturbed him on his drive, which hooked violently to the left. Having learned his lesson the day before, he tried a safe pitch-out to the fairway but swung just a little too hard and sent the ball into the rough on the opposite side. The double-bogey six pulled him back into the pack.

The scoreboard drama was watched intently by the 7,000 or so gathered around the eighteenth green, and they began to cheer as the results for the final pair were posted. While almost every golfer was being defeated by par, Jacklin made an eagle at the fifth—hitting a powerful shot with his three wood to within eight feet of the cup—to go two under on the front, and he almost made a birdie on nine. After watching

Jacklin's putt lip out, Trevino turned to his caddie and did his best imitation of Henry Longhurst, the British golf commentator: "Oh! My boy!"

Two quick birdies on the back moved Jacklin to the front of the pack. He did it mainly with putts, which he made with a style that borrowed heavily from the Palmer of old. He hunched over the ball, pressed his knees together, and made a wristy stab. This method depended on perfect timing and exquisite hand-eye coordination. On this day, Jacklin had both.

All along the course, as Sanders and Jacklin made their moves, Trevino clung steadily to par and to his good humor. At six o'clock he walked up the fourteenth fairway to find his ball on the green about fifteen feet from the hole. He quickly putted and was so certain of the result that he began to turn toward the next tee before it went in. It was his first long putt of the day, and there was a murmur in the gallery. Someone predicted that Trevino would go on a tear. He did. After making a thirty-foot putt for another birdie on fifteen, Trevino was tied for the lead at minus three.

Muirfield's sixteenth is a medium-length par three—188 yards—where all the trouble is found in bunkers. There are ten of them, positioned so tightly that any wayward shot is punished. Trevino pulled his six iron out of his bag and then laughed as the leather grip came unwound. He used a little tape from his golf bag to repair it, but his shot landed in the sand at the edge of the green.

When Trevino got to the ball, he found it was in an awkward downslope lie. He would have to hit the ball up over the four-foot-high wall of the bunker—which was made of terraced sod that looked like bricks—and then stop it before it ran past the hole, which was less than thirty feet away.

Trevino asked his caddie for "Helen," a special club he had brought from home for just this kind of shot. It was a forty-year-old ladies' wedge, designed for Wilson sporting goods by Helen Hicks, the great amateur champion of the 1930s. It was very light. It had a sharp bottom edge, and its face was marked by dimples, rather than lines. Trevino thought it would move easily through Muirfield's sand and rough and impart less spin, so the ball would land softly.

As he climbed onto the sand, Trevino hiked up his black trousers and twirled his sand wedge in his hand. He wiggled his left foot, and then his right, pushing sand away in an effort to get a secure and level stance. With his feet still moving he glanced over his shoulder to the hole, and then looked back down at the ball. He did this again, and again. Finally, with his body still shifting, he took Helen back and made a quick swing. The club, its face open, swept into the bunker, caught a bucketful of sand and the ball, and sent the whole mess high into the air. With the sand raining down on the green, the ball fell softly. It bounced once, to five feet in the air, then bounced about three feet high and came down in the tiny, inch-and-a-half space between the flagstick and the edge of the cup. Instead of struggling for par, or worse, Trevino had suddenly made a birdie with a magician's touch.

As soon as he saw the ball disappear, Trevino threw his left hand in the air and just let go of the club, sending it across the bunker, toward the crowd that ringed the green. While their cheers erupted, he stumbled backward, almost falling over. As he righted himself he reached up with his right hand to remove his baseball-style cap and then joyously slammed it to the ground. When he finally stopped twirling, he put his hands on his hips, bent backward from the waist, and let out an enormous laugh.

"If it hadn't gone in the hole," he said, "it would have gone all the way across the green!"

A stunned Tony Jacklin made his two-putt par and even managed to match Trevino's subsequent birdie on the next hole. Coming to the eighteenth, Trevino had made four birdies in a row. He turned to Willie Aitchison and said, "I'd like to make another birdie here. I've never made five birdies in a row in Great Britain, Willie."

Since only one birdie had been made at eighteen in the more than 450 rounds played thus far in the Open, Trevino was not likely to get his wish. The odds got even worse when his second shot ran through the green and rolled down a little slope and into light rough. Indeed, after he put his ball onto the putting surface, thirty feet from the hole, Jacklin was in a much better position. He was the one whom the crowd rose to cheer. They obviously suspected that with Trevino in the rough off the green, a swing of one shot or more was possible, and Jacklin might end the day alone in first.

None of this—not his errant shot, not the cheers for Jacklin—bothered Trevino as he chased after his ball. In a voice loud enough to be heard by the gallery, he sang, "Yesterday, all my troubles seemed so far away," before letting the lyrics dissolve into a tangle of words, some right, some wrong.

Here, just as at sixteen, Trevino had to stand on uneven ground. But he seemed more sure of himself and took far less time over the shot. He made a short, smooth swing. The ball jumped up, flew perhaps six or eight feet, landed on the green, and then started running toward the hole, twenty-five feet away.

Trevino, sensing that something extraordinary might happen, started running. He bolted to his right and up the crest of the slope that blocked his view. He got there just in time to see the ball follow a straight line to the hole. It hit the flagstick, rattled back to catch the edge of the cup, bounced forward again, and then fell in. Trevino threw his fist in the air, got a kiss on the cheek from his caddie, and muttered, in disbelief, "Five in a row."

Those five birdies, each achieved with shots more than twenty feet from the hole, gave the defending champion a round of 66 and, after Jacklin holed out in two, a one-shot lead as the third day of the Open turned to night. Jacklin, his brow knitted by tension, said he somehow knew his playing partner would hole that last chip. Coming off the green, Jacklin's face showed both appreciation and irritation as he clapped Trevino on the back. They would play together again the next day, in the final pairing.

In all the excitement that attended his finish on Friday, Trevino did not forget that the main drama that colored this tournament at its start—the Grand Slam quest—was not completely gone. He vowed to keep the pressure on Nicklaus. "I didn't come to Scotland to help Nicklaus win any Grand Slam," he said. "If I played golf with my wife, I'd try to beat the daylights out of her."

Trevino was wise to keep the focus on Nicklaus. Though he was a full six strokes behind, Nicklaus had made up that kind of deficit in the past. Given the conditions, and the fact that he would have no reason to hold to his cautious strategy, it was possible that tomorrow he might even break the course record. If Trevino and Jacklin both played only middling golf, Nicklaus could take his third Major in a row.

This possibility was on Nicklaus's mind as he came back to Greywalls around midnight Friday. Tom Weiskopf was with a group enjoying a drink in one of the common rooms when Nicklaus came through the oaken door. "He came in and asked what we were talking about," recalled Weiskopf, long after that night. "We said we were just talking about who would win the next day. He said, 'That's easy. I'm going to do it.' It wasn't like he was bragging. It was just how he felt. And you know what? The way he said it, it was easy to believe him."

On Saturday, as he strode to the first tee at 1:15 P.M., Jack Nicklaus believed that a score of 65 could win him his third Grand Slam title. He felt better than he had all week. His neck was free of pain and his mind was focused on attack-style golf. He chose to hit his driver. And with a gallery of several thousand crowding around, he smashed the ball so far that he needed only a nine iron to reach the green. Though he didn't get a birdie there, he scored two immediately after. On the second hole it was driver, sand wedge, six-foot putt. On the third he used a one iron and three wood to get just as close to the hole.

Playing as if he had been liberated, like Gulliver, from every restraint, Nicklaus then shaved a stroke off par on the fifth hole and found himself at the front of the number nine green in just two shots. He made a deft chip and putt to snag his fourth birdie. Dickinson, Nicklaus's stoic caddie, smiled broadly for the first time in the week and slapped him on the shoulder.

Nicklaus had gone out in just 32 shots. At this pace, he would set a new course record and, quite possibly, win the Open. The scene out on the moor became unusually frenzied and emotional, as excited Scots ran here and there to catch up with Nicklaus at each hole he played. Birdies on ten and eleven were met by roars as Nicklaus took the lead, six under par for the tournament.

A half hour behind Nicklaus, Tony Jacklin and Lee Trevino had to walk through a huge, cheering crowd to get to the first tee. The shouts were mainly for Jacklin. A record gallery of more than 22,000 had flocked to the course in hopes that he would win one for the home country. Trevino looked especially nervous, pacing back and forth while Princess Margaret, in pearls and dark glasses, looked on. It had been twenty-four years since a member of the royal family, King George VI, had witnessed the Open.

By the time they reached the fifth hole, Jacklin and Trevino knew that Nicklaus was on the move. They could hear the shouts and see that many in the gallery were leaving them and jumping ahead to get a look at what the fuss was about. "What the hell are we doing?" Trevino asked Jacklin. "Jack's going crazy up there and we're beating each other to death."

On the long fifth, Trevino lost a shot to par when he tried to use his putter—sometimes called the Texas wedge—to bounce a shot onto the green. The ball got tangled in the grass, and Trevino needed three more shots to finish. Then, on the seventh, a big, fast, frightened hare intervened, costing Trevino another bogey and helping Nicklaus to tie for the lead.

The hare in question had been startled out of his hole by the huge gallery tramping behind the seventh green. Trevino was oblivious as he stood over his par putt and the long-eared racer tore down to the fairway, then back up toward the green. As he drew the putter back, the terrified animal dashed behind him. A brown flash caught Trevino's right eye as the putter moved to strike the ball. Distracted by the brown blur, he pushed the shot, and it drifted well past the hole. The hare made another lap around the green and then, finally, made its escape through a gap in the crowd. With the miss, Trevino and Nicklaus were tied, with Jacklin one stroke behind.

The deadlock on the leaderboard didn't last. Still charging, Nicklaus gulped a lemonade on the tenth tee and then birdied the hole. He took another stroke from par on eleven. At six under, he was finally in the lead alone. For the moment it seemed possible that his furious attack on Muirfield would give him his third Major in the Slam.

Behind him, Trevino climbed to the ninth tee and turned to his caddie, Willie. "We're behind, son," he said. "Gimme that driver. We're going to make something happen." He hit his best drive of the day, an iron to the green, and a long putt for eagle. Jacklin equaled Trevino with his own eagle and they both were tied with Nicklaus.

"That will give *him* something to think about," said Trevino.

On the fifteenth tee, Nicklaus lined up his shot but was interrupted when a loud cheer announced that Jacklin had made birdie on twelve. Nicklaus set up again, only to be forced off the ball a second time by the loud response to Trevino's missed birdie putt on the same twelfth hole.

Finally, on his third try, Nicklaus had the moment of quiet he required to play. He made the green in regulation and needed to hole a six-footer—he had made several this day—for birdie. He missed. Then he came to the sixteenth, the same modest par three where Trevino had found the sand and, with Helen's help, some great good luck the day before.

On the tee, staring uphill to a narrow green, Nicklaus remembered his play here six years earlier, when he had beaten Sanders for the Open title. He had made a simple par, followed with a birdie four, and then a par on the finishing hole to win. On this day, the same performance could yield the same result—a victory—or so he thought.

Of course, thinking doesn't make it so, and there may be nothing more difficult in all of sport than repeating a fine performance on a golf course, even if it is just for three holes. This time the wind was in Nicklaus's face, and the finishing holes played longer than they had in 1966. Perhaps because of this, Nicklaus put a little too much right hand into his four iron and pulled it into a grassy bank to the left of the green. He failed to chip it close enough and suffered his first bogey of the day. Now Jacklin and Trevino held the lead without him.

Convinced that a birdie was essential, especially after losing a stroke on sixteen, Nicklaus may have tried too hard on seventeen. He pulled his drive, leaving it in the rough. As he stood over the ball, he could hear bagpipers practicing for the closing ceremony, and he knew his fate was settled. All he could do was knock the ball back onto the fairway and then go for the green with his third shot. Par was the best he could do.

As he walked up to the eighteenth green, where his ball was roughly forty feet from the hole, Nicklaus was one behind Jacklin and Trevino. The gallery understood that he was not likely to make the putt. If he scored a routine par, he would then have to depend on Trevino and Jacklin both stumbling at the end. The odds against this were great and so, it appeared, Nicklaus's valiant rush for the third title in the Grand Slam would fall one shot short.

More than 15,000 people jammed the grandstand and fairway, and they all stood and cheered Nicklaus as if he were striding toward them as the winner. Those who weren't already Nicklaus fans when the morning began had been converted as he boldly subdued the Muirfield course this day. On eighteen he used two putts to finish his record-tying round of 66. The cheering would have gone on and on if he hadn't been required to leave the green and make way for the players who followed him.

Back out on the course, Trevino was about to hit his drive on seventeen when a cameraman ran across the fairway. He backed away, then lined up again. Before he could swing, another man dashed across the course—he was carrying the cameraman's film—and Trevino stepped away a second time. He could feel his anger rise. His muscles tensed and his heart beat a little faster.

When he finally got a clear fairway, Trevino was so annoyed by the interruptions that he hooked the ball into a fairway bunker. Disgusted, he threw his driver down at Willie's feet and marched toward his ball, shaking his head and muttering to himself.

While Jacklin hit his ball to the fairway and then knocked it up near the green, Trevino entered the bunker and took such a mighty swipe at the ball that he fell over backward. The ball barely made it back to the fairway. On his third shot Trevino took a wood and sent the ball into the rough, about 128 yards short of the hole. He appeared to be cracking under the pressure. After again throwing his club, Trevino turned to Jacklin and said, "I'm through. It's all yours."

Trevino played his fourth shot as if he truly believed the match was over. He carelessly knocked it through the green, to a spot in the rough high above the hole. Lying four, to Jacklin's two, he faced a possible three-stroke swing in the score. Jacklin's pitch was weak, to about eighteen feet. Still, a birdie was possible for him, and par seemed a foregone conclusion. Even if Trevino somehow saved himself with a bogey, Jacklin would still be one shot ahead with one hole to play.

What happened next would astound everyone who saw it, and go down in history as perhaps the single most surprising turn of luck in British Open history. Though he was farther from the cup, and entitled to play first, Jacklin said, "Go ahead if you want to," and motioned for Trevino to play.

"I was steamin'," explained Trevino, recalling the event as if it occurred yesterday, rather than thirty years in the past. "Jacklin should've just let me stew in it. I was so mad I was just going to hit it and then hit it. I didn't care if I made an eight."

With a sullen face, Trevino took a nine iron in hand, quickly set up to the ball, and made an impatient swing. It was the kind of stroke he had made a thousand times as a youngster, betting nickels and dimes with other caddies. No doubt, he and the boys would fall down laughing when the occasional shot actually went in.

This time, Trevino was so sure he hit a poor shot that he started toward the ball as soon as it was struck. He knew it would stop well short of the cup. Feeling embarrassed before the whole world, he wanted to get to the ball quickly, and take another whack at it.

Jacklin paid scant attention as the ball landed. But then it kept rolling, and he and Trevino both began to focus on the little white speck and the tin cup. For an eternity it rolled, and rolled on a direct line. With its final turn, it dropped right into the cup. Without ever hitting the fairway, and having flubbed every previous shot, Trevino had slapped at the ball in disgust and put it in the hole for par. It would be hard to imagine anything more astounding.

Trevino didn't know whether to smile, or frown, or apologize. "I had been really perturbed," he explained decades later. "I was thinking I had lost the tournament, and I was so mad and so embarrassed. I just hit the ball with this totally blank feeling. When I went to the hole, I was even frowning as I got it out. Jacklin didn't say anything to me. I thought, I've got to get it together for the next hole." As they passed each other on the green, Jacklin didn't say a word.

Word of Trevino's miracle shot spread quickly to the grandstand at eighteen and was picked up immediately by the crowd milling outside the scorer's shed. Nicklaus's caddie, Jimmy, was standing outside the shed when he heard the news. He flung his vest to the ground in agony. "He holed a chip shot for a five!" he called in to Nicklaus. "What?" replied Nicklaus, disbelieving.

Trevino's chip shot had gone in on some combination of luck, instinct, and whatever swing pattern had been grooved into his mind and body through years of repetition. And no matter what anyone thought about it, the par stood. "That's the straw that broke the camel's back," he said to his caddie.

For a moment the color drained from Tony Jacklin's face. Now the pressure of the Open, and all of Britain's hopes, were upon him, and the eighteen feet between his ball and the cup must have seemed like eighteen miles. He missed his first putt, for birdie, by several feet.

"Hey, this isn't over yet!" called Trevino, to encourage him.

Jacklin then missed with his second putt. He departed the green with a bogey to Trevino's par.

Thirty years later one witness to this moment, Bruce Devlin, still empathized with what Jacklin had experienced. "For an Englishman to win the Open was a very big deal," he recalled. "The pressure was enormous. A few moments before, he felt he had that S-O-B beat. He had to be asking himself, 'What the hell is going on?'"

Though Jacklin may have already been defeated in his own heart, Trevino turned to a little Tenison Park gamesmanship to give himself an even greater psychological edge on the last hole. To reach the eighteenth tee, players had to walk up the hole's fairway. Trevino grabbed Willie by the sleeve and held him back, so that Jacklin would reach the tee first, and then be forced to wait and watch Trevino approach.

"It was a hundred-yard walk, and I didn't want to get to the tee and wait for *him*," recalled Trevino. Jacklin had plenty of time to reflect on what had happened on the seventeenth green, and fret.

When he finally arrived to take the honor of playing first, Trevino made quick work of it, giving the club two waggles and swinging before he could get nervous himself. He cracked one of the best drives he had hit all week, almost 300 yards, straight down the middle.

Among those who saw this on television was Nicklaus, who had gone to one of the club offices where a set had been tuned to the Open. "Hit a long drive, didn't he?" said Nicklaus. The TV announcer, Henry Longhurst, said, "We have seen the shot that has won the Open."

Jacklin had experienced Trevino's mind games before, in 1971, at the Piccadilly World Match-Play Championship. There Trevino had complained so much about a heckler in the crowd that Jacklin started feeling sorry for him. He lost his concentration, and the match. At Muirfield's eighteenth, Jacklin managed to shut Trevino out long enough to make a good drive. But he placed his second shot in a bunker to the right of the green. Trevino's second rolled straight at the pin, ending up six feet past it.

Despite the loud, grateful cheers he heard as he reached the grandstand, Tony Jacklin was the picture of defeat as he entered the greenside bunker. His shot out was serviceable and professional, but not good enough to make a par possible. For him, the Open was over.

As he walked onto the green, Trevino took off his hat, waved to the crowd, and then stared straight up to the sky, as if he were thanking the heavens for what had happened to him in the last fifteen minutes. Jacklin rolled his putt, Trevino begged it to fall—"Get in! Get in! Get in!"—but the ball was as drained of energy as Jacklin. It stopped a foot short of the goal. Jacklin made bogey, letting Nicklaus into second place, and falling back to third.

With two putts Trevino won. His total of 278 was four better than the lowest score posted in eleven Opens at Muirfield. He accepted an embrace from his caddie and the two of them waltzed for a moment on the green. His prize check—$14,000 worth of British pound sterling—was less than he won from the bets he had placed on himself in local shops. His acceptance speech was brief, the sort of rushed statement a man might make when he's afraid his hosts will change their minds. "All the words of encouragement that Jack gave me in the past couple of years finally paid off," he said. "He probably wishes he kept his mouth shut."

Jack Nicklaus was among the first to congratulate Trevino, who consoled him on the end to the Grand Slam bid. After the closing ceremonies Nicklaus then rushed back to Greywalls, laced on his sneakers, and played pounding tennis for a good long time. It no doubt helped to take his mind off his loss of the Open and his great dream. But the relief was only temporary. Nicklaus would return to the 1972 Open at Muirfield many times, in his mind, and wonder.

One shot—the margin that Nicklaus lost by—is an even slimmer margin when you consider that it came after four days of play against the toughest field in the world. It was all that prevented him from pulling off one of the greatest feats in sport. Eventually he would decide that he had been right about the three finishing holes on the last day of play. If he had scored as well as he had in 1966—three, four, and four—he would have won whether Trevino had made his chip on seventeen or not.

Many years later, Nicklaus would recall with some emotion how the Scottish gallery had encouraged him, perhaps even loved him along during that final round. Normally reserved and even stingy with their applause, the Scots had made it clear that no matter the outcome, Nicklaus had joined Jones in their hearts. It all helped, but long afterward Nicklaus would confess, in his memoirs, that even love couldn't overcome all his pain. In 1998 he wrote: ". . . the frustration and disappointment were more intense than I care to remember, even now, a quarter century later."

Over time, as he looked back at Muirfield and the Open, Trevino concluded that the tournament had been won during the third round, when his bunker shot went in the hole. "I realized then that there was less pressure on me, the defending champion, because you just aren't expected to repeat," he said thirty years later. Nicklaus, with his pursuit of the Grand Slam, and Jacklin, with the weight of Britain's pride on his back, were under far greater burdens.

A record crowd of more than 84,000 people witnessed the Grand Slam Open, which decades later would be remembered as one of the most dramatic Majors ever played. Many who competed that year eventually won an Open themselves.

Tom Weiskopf, who would win the title the very next year, finished in seventh position, eight strokes back, alongside Arnold Palmer. Gary Player was a stroke better than Weiskopf in 1972. He would also win a future Open, his third, in 1974. Johnny Miller could do no better than a 75 on the last day at Muirfield, and ended up in a tie for thirteenth. But he would win the tournament himself in 1976, at Royal Birkdale.

Tony Jacklin would never contend in another Major championship. Most observers agreed that after Muirfield he was never the same competitor. The greatest moment in his professional life after Muirfield came in 1987, when he served as captain of the first European team to take the Ryder Cup in a match played on American soil. Great Britain's golf fans felt as much pride in this accomplishment as they had when Jacklin almost won the Open back in 1972.

Doug Sanders would not challenge for the British Open title ever again. He would eventually retire from the game as one of the greatest players who never won a Major. (He would finish in second place five times.) But every time he crossed the Atlantic, even just to play some casual golf on the old links, he would be met with outpourings of love and admiration. His nerve, his honesty, and even his failings bound him forever to Scots, who understood both the nature of the game and its players.

In his account of the 1972 Open, the *London Observer*'s great golf writer Peter Dobereiner reported that one of Muirfield's members had said, after the tournament, that Trevino's finish had been impossible. American pro Dave Marr, who heard the remark in passing, stopped to explain. "You forget, sir," he said, "that God is a Mexican." In a later column Dobereiner would declare the 1972 event the greatest Open ever played. "How are we going to follow Muirfield?" he wondered.

The timeless comfort of Muirfield and the Open slipped away as the competitors from the American tour packed for their flights home. If, while in Scotland, they had paid any attention at all to events outside golf, they would have known that Northern Ireland was boiling over, again. Even as the Open players were leaving Prestwick, more than a thousand British troops were arriving in Belfast. In the week to come, thirty-six people would die in sectarian violence.

In the United States, newspapers reported that President Nixon was fighting efforts to press the probe into Watergate. Henry Kissinger's secret peace talks with North Vietnam were revealed even as Republican senators began to join those demanding an unconditional withdrawal from the war. In the field, the South Vietnamese had still not pushed the North out of Quangtri. One of the most disturbing photo images of the war—a picture of a naked girl, a terrified victim of napalm bombs, fleeing a combat scene—was published in papers coast-to-coast.

Everywhere, it seemed, the sense of order and basic assumptions about society were falling apart. In the first week after the British Open competitors came home, the terrible Tuskegee scandal, in which the government denied medical treatment to black men infected with syphilis, was exposed. On the same day, Thomas Eagleton's history of depression became public. It would be used to force him to resign as the Democratic Party's candidate for vice president.

CHAPTER 8

There is nothing really exceptional about
Gary's game, except his desire to win.
−Jack Nicklaus on Gary Player

It's quite possible that Lee Trevino got nearly as much attention for stopping the Grand Slam as Jack Nicklaus would have received had he achieved it. As soon as he won the British Open at Muirfield, Trevino was besieged by the media. (Even the newsmagazines ran full features on his win.) He further inflamed their interest by doing and saying the unexpected at every turn.

Before leaving Great Britain, Trevino made it clear that unlike Nicklaus, who seemed obsessed with history and Major championships, he was in it mainly for the money. Talking as fast as ever, he told the press he intended to amass $1 million in winnings by 1974−a quicker pace of earnings than even Nicklaus−and then retire to dusty El Paso, where he would sit on his bales of cash. "I'm going to play as much as I can, as hard as I can, win all I can by age forty," he told the press. "I ain't gonna be out here trying to hack it around and beat the hungry kids.

"And I sure as hell ain't gonna be a pro at some club somewhere and stand around sweating and saying, 'Yes, Mr. Moneybags' and 'No, Mrs. Fat Thing,' and listen to them yell: 'I don't like my starting time' or 'What's wrong with this cart?' or 'Boy, I need some help on my swing.' "

Once Trevino got going, he tended to keep on going. In this case he went on to explain that big tournament wins had led him to business opportunities even more lucrative than the tour. At the moment he was building a huge apartment village, constructing a thirty-six-hole golf course complex, and hawking everything from soda pop to cars. According to one press account he had three big land development deals going, one worth $10 million.

Though the idea that a pro golfer making big money would retire at age forty sounded odd, Trevino was just saying the sort of things that others, including Nicklaus and Player, said in private. They also thought about quitting the tour and focusing on their business interests. Nicklaus could have easily kept busy working full-time on just one of his projects, the new golf course and subdivision called Muirfield, which he was constructing outside Columbus. But only Trevino had the nerve to let the public in on the fact that big money waited for golf's champions long after retirement.

He was also exceptionally candid, intentionally or not, about the burdens of fame. When he returned to the States, Trevino was a guest on *The Tonight Show with Johnny Carson,* which was still being broadcast from New York City. He got drunk before getting to the studio, and even before he went on stage began flirting with Elaine Stritch, an actress who was also booked to appear on the Carson show.

In those days TV networks stocked the lounges where guests were kept waiting with plenty of liquor. The way Trevino would remember it, before Stritch went on, she dropped the dress she had arrived in to the floor and wriggled into a new one. This only encouraged his flirting. He poured a double cognac and watched her banter with Carson until he was called onto the set. After struggling past the curtain, the British Open champ tripped and almost fell onto his host. "Oh my God!" said Carson as Trevino stumbled toward him.

Once Trevino was seated, the conversation that ensued included remarks about Mexican elevator operators and Trevino propositioning Stritch in front of a national audience.

Trevino had made a fool of himself with America watching, but he wasn't through acting out. After the show he had a few more drinks at his hotel and began to feel truly depressed and deeply exhausted. He wanted to get away from the fans, the press, the business deals, and the tour. Forgetting about the tournament he was committed to play, he got in his car and started driving south, in the direction of home.

Before sleep overwhelmed him, Trevino managed to steer his car off the New Jersey Turnpike and into a motel parking lot. He checked in and fell into bed. He awoke in the middle of the next afternoon, not knowing where he was. He called his wife and she dialed back, to get the name of the place and the town where her husband had fallen to Earth. She then instructed him to make his way back to Newark Airport where a ticket for a flight home was waiting.

Years later, a sober Trevino would guess that his experience after the British Open was more than a matter of alcohol and fatigue. It was the kind of emotional crisis people call a nervous breakdown. A vacation with Claudia steadied his mood, but all the stress that came with being a winner, with being the man who stopped Nicklaus, remained.

Though the majority of America's best golfers had been overseas at the British Open, the PGA Tour had nevertheless held a tournament that week. The Milwaukee Open was won by Jim Colbert, a journeyman in his eighth year as a pro. Buddy Allin played some of his best golf of the year—four rounds in the 60s—and finished just one stroke behind the champion, in second place. He won $8,531 and jumped to number forty on the tour's money list. It was certain that he would reach his goal for the year: a spot in the top sixty and full playing privileges for the next season.

A week later, Gene Littler, who had lost so much muscle to the surgeon's knife that lifting his arm was difficult, found his way back into pro golf. In the twelve weeks since his cancer operation, Littler had trained his body to compensate for the missing tissue. In his debilitated state, Littler had found the kind of grind-it-out determination that many people thought he had lacked when he was whole. He had worked with a physical therapist and followed that with his own weight training, swimming, and practice tee sessions. At first he had to struggle to stay patient, but as he saw progress his anxiety eased.

His return to competition came at a minor professional

event in Lancaster, Pennsylvania. It was a one-day, so-called mini-tournament, but the field boasted more than a dozen PGA Tour winners, including Doug Sanders, Jerry Heard, Johnny Miller, and Billy Casper. Littler's grit and rebuilt swing produced a score of 69, which won the day. In fact, he was the only one to beat par on a difficult course. He modestly credited the performance to lucky "chipping and putting." But he also said he'd be ready to try one of the main events of the big tour by summer's end.

Though it was only July, the end of the Nicklaus crusade and the rapid approach of the final Major—the PGA Championship—made it seem as if the golf year were coming to a close. The last Major event would be held in Michigan at Oakland Hills Country Club, just eighteen days after Trevino collected the winner's check at Muirfield. Trevino was full of bravado as the tournament approached, announcing that he would book two airline seats home from the championship, one for himself and one for the trophy.

In contrast with Trevino's swagger, Gary Player would enter the PGA Championship irritated and defensive. He was having a good year, if not a great one, with his victory in New Orleans and more than enough earnings—$74,004—to be ranked number sixteen on the American tour. But this was a pale performance for a superstar, and one sportswriter had publicly challenged the idea that Player belonged to the so-called Big Three—Nicklaus, Palmer, Player—of the sport. Prideful and ever sensitive to his image, Player was hurt by such comments. He considered himself to be, at age thirty-six, in his prime, and worthy of greater respect. After all, his record of victories and earnings from tournament golf was second only to Nicklaus's.

In the short time between Majors, Nicklaus took much of the excitement out of the one significant event in golf that was scheduled, the National Team Championship at Arnold Palmer's home course in Ligonier, Pennsylvania. In the previous two years, Nicklaus had paired with Palmer to drub dozens of teams comprised of many of the world's best players. The four-round tournament was played in a best-ball format, with the lowest score from each team posted on each hole. The Nicklaus/Palmer team had been a delight for spectators, something like DiMaggio and Williams together at an All-Star game.

This year, to the gallery's disappointment, instead of appearing at Laurel Valley Country Club, Nicklaus was pictured on America's sports pages showing his right hand wrapped in heavy bandages. A scratch he had barely noticed when it occurred had become so infected that it required surgery. With just a week to go before the first round, Nicklaus was in danger of missing the PGA Championship altogether. At the very least, he would come to the course without much preparation.

The PGA, with a long history of upsets and surprise winners, had to be the quirkiest Major, the one least dominated by the superstars of the game. In the 1950s, half the champions were men with names such as Harper, Turnesa, Hebert, Burkemo, and Harbert, who would never win another Major. In the 1960s, Gary Player and Jack Nicklaus each won a PGA title, but so did Dave Marr, Al Geiberger, and Bobby Nichols. Not one in this second group would ever claim another Major.

No one understood the unpredictable nature of this tournament better than Palmer. It was the only Major he had never conquered, though he had finished second three times. At the 1964 PGA Championship he became the first player to shoot four consecutive rounds below 70, but he still lost to Bobby Nichols. In 1970, Palmer had chased Dave Stockton through the final round. Stockton played like the Palmer of old, spraying shots into sand and water, only to make dramatic recoveries. Upon capturing the only Major of his career, Stockton had said, "I felt sorry for Arnold for about one millionth of a second." In 1972, Palmer would approach the PGA Championship as his most important goal. "I'd feel like I'd left something undone," he said about failing to capture this title.

The PGA Championship had been much less troublesome for Nicklaus than it had been for Palmer. He had won in 1963 and again in 1971. The tournament was played in 1971 at Palm Beach Gardens, Florida, just minutes from Nicklaus's home. He would recall it as one of the weirdest victories in his career, one that came despite erratic play and depended on a putting lesson from his friend Deane Beman. But with it, Nicklaus became the first man to win every one of the game's Majors twice. That had been something to shoot for.

Nicklaus would defend his title in suburban Detroit on a course that Ben Hogan named "the Monster" when he won the U.S. Open there in 1951. Built in 1918 according to a Donald Ross design, the South Course at Oakland Hills Country Club was redesigned as a Major championship course in 1950 by Robert Trent Jones. Concerned that power players had overwhelmed many layouts, Trent Jones tried to require accuracy from the big hitters. He made the landing areas for tee shots small, and defended them with bunkers, water, and rough. Each green was contoured to provide small collection points where the cup could be located. Shots that missed these spots would tend to roll away from the hole, not toward it.

Players who came to Oakland Hills complained long and loud about its difficulty, but the course was deemed a masterpiece that rewarded intelligence and patience. Both of these virtues had been on display at the last Major played at Oakland Hills, the 1961 U.S. Open, which was won by Gene Littler. But even he could not break par for the tournament. Indeed, in four different U.S. Opens at Oakland Hills no one, not even Hogan, had bested par.

Though his sutures denied him the chance to practice, Nicklaus could prepare his mind and his heart, which, given his defeat in Scotland, were probably more damaged than his hand. In the days before the final Major it was clear that he was searching for a way to make the challenge meaningful. Eventually he settled on the idea of an "American Slam," meaning victories in the Masters, the U.S. Open, and the PGA Championship. "Nobody's ever done that, have they?" he asked. He was right. No one had.

But while the possibility of an American Slam may have helped get Nicklaus fired up, it didn't move the press. With Trevino taking the title in Muirfield, interest in big-league golf waned. In the end, only 75 of the 200 writers who had applied for credentials to cover the PGA Championship would actually show up.

No one outside his friends and family paid attention to how Buddy Allin prepared for the 1972 PGA Championship. For the record, he spent some time with one of his closest friends on tour, Al Geiberger, who gave him a lesson on chipping. (He had reminded Allin that he needed to hit the ball harder when a chip had to roll against the grain of the grass.) Allin then went home to Santa Barbara to consult with Jim Judd. Besides working at the post office, Judd had been the pro at the municipal course where Allin had learned to play. Allin trusted that Judd was a good teacher and, more important, a good enough friend to assess his swing and offer the right advice in the right manner. Like a good physician, Judd would first "do no harm," meaning he would do nothing to plant doubts in Allin's mind. But he would also be able to correct whatever flaws had crept into his prize student's game.

It worked. Bumping along in near privacy—the record 19,300 first-round fans were chasing Trevino, Nicklaus, Player, and Palmer—Allin birdied the long number two hole and then used his new chipping technique to get up and down from the fringe in two shots on numbers four, eight, and nine. He came to the seventeenth hole tied for the first-round lead. No one in the gallery or the press corps had any idea he was playing so well because for some reason his score had not been posted on any of the boards on the course.

At 201 yards, the seventeenth at Oakland Hills required

a precise and straight shot into a green protected by five bunkers in the front and one in the back. The hole was made even longer by the fact that the green was elevated a full thirty feet above the teeing area. A Nicklaus could hit a high, soft-landing, medium iron shot that would clear the front bunkers and stop before rolling into the one in the back. But a short-hitter like Allin had to take a long iron, or even a wood. These clubs were much harder to hit high and straight and soft. Undaunted, Allin hit his trusty Wilson five wood to the green, and then he sank a long putt for birdie.

Coming to eighteen, Allin faced a 453-yard hole that members played to a par five but the pros had to make in four. It was a long uphill haul into the wind, and out of 139 men who would try on this day, only four would get on the green in two. Allin did it with his five wood, and got the ball into the hole with two putts. No one knew he had taken the lead, with a score of 68, until he was already in the locker room. When at last his name was put atop the leaderboard, the most often uttered phrase in the gallery became, "Who is that guy?"

Allin, who had never before played in a PGA Championship, posted his score early in the day, and one by one the stars of the PGA Tour were unable to match him. Palmer had one of his best rounds of the year, careening around the course in his daredevil style of old. He made five birdies, but also four bogeys. On four different holes he needed three shots to get his ball in the hole from the fringe around the green. In this way, a potentially spectacular round became merely good. His 69 placed him in a tie for second place, alongside Jerry Heard and a few others. Lagging behind were Gary

Player with a 71, Nicklaus with a 72, and Lee Trevino with a 73.

This was how the first-day scores added up—with Allin alone in first place—until the very last player on the course, someone less well known even than the front-runner, reached the eighteenth green. Stan Thirsk wasn't even a touring professional. He was the club pro at the Kansas City Country Club. But he was good enough to be putting for birdie, and full possession of first, as the sun set at Oakland Hills. He missed, settled for a tie with Allin, and then went to the pressroom to apologize to the assembled writers for making them miss their dinners to rewrite their reports.

It's rare for a long shot to scoot to the top of a Major and stay there, and Buddy Allin certainly didn't expect it. Decades later he tried to explain how he felt. "I looked at it this way; I had played one very good round on a very tough golf course. That score meant I was probably going to make the cut in my first PGA Championship, and get paid that week. My first battle was to make the cut. That was my focus."

Away from the golf course, Allin was focused on the most basic challenges of supporting his wife, Cecilia, and their son, Aaron, both materially and emotionally. His marriage was not going well. In recent months Cecilia and her closest friend, who happened to be married to Allin's best friend, had been reading feminist books and *Ms.* magazine and adopting new attitudes on men and women, marriage and family.

"I remember hearing a lot of Carly Simon songs," recalled

Allin, with a smile. "And there was that other one that goes, 'I am woman, hear me roar.' "

Of course, the songs were just emblems for issues that many women discussed often. Allin recalls that most of all, his wife wanted an identity larger than that of being the wife of a pro golfer. "She did not want to be Mrs. Somebody," said Allin. "More and more she wanted to be her own person, not just someone who supported me. The tension around all that was building that summer of '72. I tried to understand what she was saying, but it was a different time. The traditional marriage was still something most people did."

Private struggles and inner demons can ruin a man on the golf course. On the second day of the PGA Championship, Allin was probably affected most by self-doubt. Eager to get off to a good start, he played poorly off the first tee and never recovered the magic he had possessed the day before. He made a 77, though he would remember it feeling like an 87. He fell out of contention, but did make the cut. Thirsk was even worse. He carded an 82 and survived the cut by a single stroke.

On the second day, as the surprise leaders met their not-so-surprising fates, some more prominent names rose. Allin's close friend, fellow Californian Jerry Heard, took the lead with an even-par round and a two-day total of just one under. In his fourth year on tour, Heard was becoming a popular player with the galleries and a serious contender for titles. A victory in March at the Citrus Open, combined with a flurry of top-ten finishes, had made him number three in tour winnings, just behind Trevino and Nicklaus. But it was more his manner than his play that endeared him to fans. Heard's love for the game showed on his boyish face. He wore his hair long, and his shirts untucked, and he always seemed to be grinning.

"I was never going to give a stroke away to anyone because of temperament," said Heard, long after his tour days were over. "I got along with people and was able to learn a lot. Trevino, he knew a whole lot about the swing. He helped me switch from a draw to a fade. A lot of amateurs like a draw because it goes farther. But a professional doesn't need the distance. You want to get it in there soft, and a fade will do that."

Like many younger players of the era, Heard was a bit awed by Arnold Palmer and Jack Nicklaus–Palmer because he was a living legend and Nicklaus because he was so good. He felt closer to Trevino because "he had a little 'I don't give a shit' about him, and I liked that."

On the second day of the PGA, Heard was paired with Palmer. He admired him, but he knew that the old champion was on the downslope of his career. "He could still rip it, but it takes four days of good scores to win and that's a lot harder when you're older," he said. "I didn't think he had much of a chance anymore, at the Majors." On this day, Heard was right. As he made lots of fine putts and pushed his chip shots close to the hole, Palmer was leaving them short of the hole or running them past it. From a 69 on Thursday, Palmer fell to a 75 on Friday.

"I'm just sick and tired of my golf," he said when it was over. "It's just awful and I'm very disgusted. But it seems like I can't do any better than what I've been doing."

As Palmer fell by the wayside, Jim Jamieson took up the

chase, pulling within one shot. Jamieson was suffering from a slightly sprained wrist, but it didn't seem to affect him much. The pressroom crowd was pulling for Jamieson because he had brought a case of champagne to Michigan and was promising them a party if he won. At the end of his second round Trevino was also upbeat. He had bettered his first-day score and was still in contention, five out.

No longer in contention was Nicklaus, who had recorded a 72 in his opening round but fell to a 75 on Friday. Lumbering behind several club pros, he seemed uninspired and out of sorts. His drives flew crooked, his irons were erratic, and his putts wouldn't fall. "For some reason," he would lament, "I just didn't have it in me." The reason was back in Scotland, in the ruins of his Grand Slam campaign.

The scores were inflated at Oakland Hills because the rough—saturated in the days before the tournament by torrential rains—had grown so thick and high it resembled a spring alfalfa crop. Many players were also baffled by Oakland Hills's greens, which undulated so severely they could give a man vertigo. Add the pressure of it being the last two rounds of a Major, and the scores would likely go even higher.

On Saturday the pressure got to Jerry Heard on the ninth hole. Normally calm and unflappable, Heard was distracted by the click of a photographer's camera. But instead of backing away from his tee shot, he stayed with it, sending the ball astray. The photographer tagged along, and Heard stayed angry. He couldn't resist complaining, and an argument ensued, with the photographer saying he was simply doing his job and

Heard pointing out that he was doing the same. He made bogey, and followed that with another at fourteen when he missed from three feet. His 72 was a fine score, but the trend was in the wrong direction.

Gary Player, meanwhile, was moving in the right direction. Having dealt with death threats and charging mobs in the past, Player was barely affected by the tension associated with the third day at an ordinary Major. He had also reached two important conclusions about the championship. He was certain that matters would not be settled until the back nine on Sunday. Until then, he needed only to stay close to the lead. Second, he believed that the best-conditioned athlete would be the winner. This was because the PGA was the last of the Majors, and most pros were bone-tired. Since he considered himself the fittest man in golf—and he was probably right—Player was confident that he would have the energy needed to play his best.

With his tendency toward hyperbole, it was hard to tell whether Player meant it when he said that the Oakland Hills course was the toughest he had seen in America, but the strategy he used suggested it was. To help him stay in the fairways, he hit very few woods, even on the tees. And even though the greens were soft and receptive, he went after the pins only a few times. With this steady approach he made five birdies and two bogeys to match the lowest score posted so far, a 67. His work on the greens was superb, as four times he rolled in putts of twenty-five to thirty feet.

Eight other pros broke 70 on Saturday. Nicklaus was among them, at 68, but there were so many players ahead of him he admitted that it was too little, too late. (His goal had been to break the course record of 65.) The real challenge to Player would come, ironically, from the least-fit man in the field, Jim Jamieson.

After the third round of the tournament, Gary Player ran a mile or two on the streets near his hotel before going to bed. On Sunday morning he awoke homesick and, after calculating the cost of the call in his head, asked the hotel operator to connect him with South Africa. He wanted to talk to his wife, Vivienne, and to his father, Henry, who was then seventy-three years old.

Superficially, Henry and Gary Player couldn't have been more different. Gary, or "Geddy" as South Africans said it, was short and sinewy. He was also handsome and worldly and rich. IIis father, tall, stout, and putty-faced, had been a miner on an hourly wage all of his adult life. He was an exceedingly tough man—his nickname was Whiskey—who had worked a mile below the surface of the earth and had gone into debt to finance his son's golf career. But he was also his son's harshest critic. The way Gary talked about him, it sounded like Whiskey Player provoked in his son love, fear, anger, and pride, sometimes all at once.

Despite their differences, Player the son was, even at age thirty-six, deferential and deeply grateful to his father. When, on that Sunday morning, Henry said, "Son, please win it for me," Gary answered, "I will."

Many of Player's fellow pros, who understood that Player carried extra political burdens, were pulling for him. When he got to his locker he opened it to find a handwritten note from Chi Chi Rodriguez. "Take it all. I want you to win," it read.

It would be impossible to say which weighed more heavily on Player as he appeared on the first tee in the last group to play on Sunday. First there was the obvious stress that comes to the leader on the final day of a Major championship. Then there was his own ambition, a competitive drive that was so strong it amazed even the likes of Nicklaus. Finally there was Henry Player's plea and Geddy's promise. Add them all together, and the weight of expectations would bring anyone to his knees.

With a chill wind blowing and a light rain falling, Player responded, humanly enough, by putting his approach shot on number one into a bunker—a striking error for one of the best iron players in the game—and struggling just to get a bogey. A twenty-five-foot putt netted him a birdie on the second hole, but then he gave away a shot to par on number three, and another on number four. Having given away his lead, he steadied himself with six pars.

Up ahead of Player, the rest of the field jockeyed for position. At various moments one or another of seven different men—including Heard, Casper, Sanders, and Jamieson—shared first place. Almost all of them stumbled as they began the fateful back nine. Sanders made four bogeys in a row and was out of it. Casper made three and never recovered. Heard got into even more trouble on his way to a final score of 74.

The exception was Jamieson. The anti-Player—well over 200 pounds and often filled with beer—had awakened with a sore throat to go with his sore and swollen wrist. But even in this condition, he played Oakland Hills with the precision it demanded. Three birdies against no bogeys brought Jamieson to the sixteenth tee at level par for the tournament and one shot ahead of Player. It also brought him to a level of nervousness he could not control. His mind was filled with a thousand hopes and dreads.

"I was thinking about how, if I won, I'd have a lifetime exemption to play on the tour," recalled Jamieson. "I was thinking about how much money it was worth in endorsements, how it would change my life."

On the sixteenth hole Jamieson hit a solid drive, but his second shot spun off the green. A chip and two putts gave him a bogey and placed him back in a tie with Player. Then, as he reached the seventeenth, he discovered a member of the gallery, a very large, very loud, very drunk man, had taken up residence beneath a tree next to the tee. It took twenty minutes—which allowed Jamieson far too much time for reflection—for police to arrive and finally remove the drunk.

A low-ball hitter, Jamieson would have found the tee shot on this long, uphill par three a challenge under any circumstance, but on the last day of the PGA Championship the hill he faced looked like a mountain. He took out a two iron (hardly his favorite club) and hit the ball on a straight line, directly into the slope. The ball buried in the turf. His pitch didn't land close to the hole, and he two-putted for another bogey.

"By this time I'm sure I wasn't worried about Gary Player or anyone else," said Jamieson. "I'm sure I was just worried about myself going into that finishing hole."

Eighteen, which had given so many players so much trouble all week, did it to Jamieson. He hit a nearly perfect drive, but he had so much adrenaline pumping through his body that he then smashed a five iron right over the green. A chip was followed by a miss on a short putt. He had his third bogey in a row and could only hope that Player would falter into a play-off.

Gary Player could hardly have done more to raise Jamieson's hopes. A terrible drive on fourteen brought a bogey there and on fifteen he missed a putt of less than two feet to lose another stroke to par. His lead was down to a single stroke when he got up on the sixteenth tee. Sixteen at Oakland Hills may be the second-most difficult hole on a course comprised of eighteen difficult holes. It's a shortish par four of 409 yards. But the fairway, with trees on both sides, bends from left to right at a severe angle. The small green is fronted by a large pond that cannot be skirted.

The only play from the tee is to the left. Player pushed the ball right, landing in the rough behind some tall spreading willow trees. The pond lay past the trees, in front of the green. The only reasonable play would be a punch shot back to the fairway, where Player could hope to salvage par. But he wanted more.

"I really felt like it was do or die," he would say long afterward. "I mean, the only ones who care if you finish second are yourself and your dog. I wanted to be first, always. I wanted the championship."

What happened next was so unlikely and so grand that years later many people who couldn't possibly have witnessed the event would insist they were there. In truth, the number of witnesses was probably fewer than a thousand. And many of them were, like Player himself, unable to see the complete flight of what became known as The Shot.

As was his custom, Player was dressed in black pants and black shirt, and the color seemed quite appropriate as he approached the ball. "I was really demoralized," he would say later. "I was this close, but it was slipping away."

The green and the flag were not visible from the high grass where Player found his ball, so he walked forward through the trees. When he finally caught sight of the green, he spotted a man in a folding chair positioned just high enough in the background to be seen from where he would play. This would be his target.

Back at the ball, Player's caddie told him the distance to the pin—150 yards—most of it over water. Normally Player might choose a seven iron or even a six to cover that distance. But he needed the loft of a nine iron to get the ball up high enough to clear the trees that towered in front of him. A typical nine-iron shot would travel just 110 or 120 yards, though, which in this case was somewhere in the middle of the pond.

Small as he was, Player owned a powerful swing. If he could swing as hard as he possibly could, and keep steady enough to make the ball travel straight, he might reach the green with the nine iron. He pulled the nine from the bag. The caddie stepped back. Player set himself in an extra wide stance, to maintain his balance. His backswing was a bit exaggerated, to build more torque in his midsection; when he brought the club down into the ball it made a divot that was more than a foot long.

When the ball cleared the trees, it seemed to hang there like a paper moon tacked to a playhouse curtain. With his view blocked by the trees, Player began to run to his left toward the open fairway, where he might see the green. Behind him, the gallery began running, too. Player couldn't move fast enough to see the ball land softly and spin to a stop just four feet from the hole. But the cheers let him know that he had done something remarkable.

It was one of the best swings anyone ever made with a golf club. The immediate result was that a disaster was turned into an easy birdie putt, which he made. Player, the man the press had written out of the Big Three, was on his way to another Major victory. On seventeen he made a chip and putt for par. On eighteen he hit perhaps his longest, straightest drive of the day and made a par to win by two. His final score, 281, was one over par for the tournament.

That night, after accepting the trophy and the check and making more long-distance calls, he was left to savor it. A solitary Player ran in the darkness, holding to his fitness routine and feeling full of gratitude. "I took stock of my life," he said. "And I said to myself, 'You are blessed.' "

After he won, Player extended his stay in America to compete in the World Series of Golf, which he won by two strokes over Nicklaus, Trevino, and Gay Brewer. He would finish the year seventh on the money list with $120,719 in earnings, three victories, and seven top-ten finishes. Outside the United States, he won the South African Open, the Japan Airlines Open, and the Brazilian Open.

With nine top tens, Arnold Palmer won a little less than $84,000. This was enough to place him twenty-fifth on the end-of-year rankings, but this was hardly a Palmer-size achievement. In 1972, for the first time since 1955, Palmer failed to win a tournament in a full season on the PGA Tour. All in all, it was his worst year ever, and many of the troops in his army feared it signaled the end of his competitive days. Palmer did, too.

After the PGA Championship, Lee Trevino won the Greater Hartford Open, beating Lee Elder in a play-off and denying him the automatic Masters invitation that a tour victory provided. Trevino also won the St. Louis Open, which gave him four wins on the year. His $218,805 in winnings was enough to qualify him for second place at year's end. His steady good play won him the Vardon Trophy for the lowest per-round average on tour. This seemingly consistent record obscured the fact that he still struggled with success. His troubles boiled over into public view at the Sahara Invitational. Feeling burned out and frustrated by slow play, he picked up his ball and walked off the course in the middle of the third round.

"We took three hours and ten minutes to play the first nine holes," explained Trevino decades later. "I couldn't stand it anymore and just picked my ball up and walked off. I remember one of the tour officials—he always called me Pinto Bean—came to me and said, 'Pinto Bean, you gotta tell me you were sick or something.' I guess I was, sort of. But really I had just had enough."

The Sahara Open turned out to be notable for one other reason. It produced the first victory for Lanny Wadkins, who would be Rookie of the Year and heralded as a future star.

Wadkins and all the other up-and-coming young players saw Nicklaus as a role model. Through the end of 1972, Nicklaus showed them how the best player in the world responds to the end of a dream. After he lost the Grand Slam and the PGA Championship he set a new goal, to become the first man to win $300,000 in a year on tour. (In fact, he won $320,942, which was more than $100,000 over what his nearest rival won.) He clinched his goal by winning the final event of the year, the Walt Disney World Open. It was his seventh victory of the year, a capstone on a yearlong performance that won him Player of the Year honors and heralded the Nicklaus Decade. No season, however, brought him more success than 1972. He would never win as much money as he did that year, and only once, in 1973, would he equal the seven tournament titles he captured in 1972.

In 1972, Jack Nicklaus came as close to making the sweep in a single year as any man since Jones. He dominated the first two Majors and lost at Muirfield by a single stroke. Who knows what would have happened if he had gone to Oakland Hills with that third title in hand? As it was, a less than inspired performance brought him within four shots of that title, too.

But consider what would have been lost in a Nicklaus sweep. If the Slam had been completed, the golf world would have been denied Trevino's most unlikely victory in British Open history. His display of gamesmanship, personality, and talent became synonymous with the Open's history of surprise. More significant, his chip-ins and steadfast play under pressure came to illustrate the almost mystical combination of talent and fate that is the ancient game.

If Nicklaus had somehow prevailed in the Slam, golf would not have Gary Player's shot at Oakland Hills's sixteenth hole to savor through time. The Shot would be remembered as one of the finest swings made under pressure in the long history of golf. It became the signature moment in Gary Player's long, successful career.

The successes of Player and Trevino meant that the dramatic possibility of Nicklaus's Grand Slam pursuit was replaced by a story that became far more exciting. And in failing to reach his goal, Nicklaus may have become more human in the public's mind. Admiration for his character joined the sense of awe many felt about his talents. And the tour season of 1972 would be cherished for decades to come.

POSTSCRIPT

Brian "Buddy" Allin's family odyssey through the American golf tour ended in 1973 when he and his newly feminist wife decided to divorce. The decision followed his victory at the Citrus Open, which he remembered with some humor: "She followed me from the tee, walking on the right side if I drove it right, down the left side if I went left. We were fighting. I didn't want her near me. So I hit it down the middle every time. That's how I won."

Allin would claim three more titles on the regular tour before retiring in 1981, after a bout with melanoma on his leg. (His second wife served him with papers as he emerged from anesthesia after surgery.) He remained in the golf business, working for a club manufacturer and as a club pro. He played five seasons of the Senior PGA Tour, winning the 1997 American Express Invitational, and authored a book on the swing titled *Center-line*.

Alice Cooper continued to perform for three decades, even as younger musicians developed more outrageous acts.

By the 1990s he had become an avid, some might say addicted, golfer of real ability. He would even play in the Pebble Beach tournament.

Bruce Crampton won fourteen times on the PGA Tour before joining the Senior Tour in 1986. He immediately became that tour's leading money winner. He won seven times that first year, twenty times overall as a senior.

After retiring from tournament golf in the late 1990s, Crampton made news again in the year 2000 by making public a lifelong battle with clinical depression. In an article he wrote he explained that his father and two uncles had committed suicide, and that he had fought the illness most of his playing life. Medication and an end to competition seemed to be his cure.

In 2001, Crampton opened a high-tech swing analysis center in Annapolis, Maryland. Based on a new discipline called "motion capture," it uses multiple cameras to provide imaging of movement. When it's not being used by athletes, Crampton lends the facility to medical researchers.

Lee Elder went back to South Africa with Gary Player several times after 1972. He became a figure of racial outreach both at home and abroad. His stature influenced a change in the rules that opened the Masters to every player who won on the PGA Tour.

Elder won the Monsanto Open in 1974, which earned him an invitation to the Masters in 1975. Though he missed the cut, in part because of the hoopla around his breaking the race barrier, Elder would return to Augusta five more times. His best finish was seventeenth, in 1979. Until a golfer named Tiger Woods came along in 1996, Elder was the most successful African American in the history of the PGA Tour.

Elder won eight times on the Senior PGA Tour and continued to compete occasionally into the year 2001.

Jerry Heard, who finished fifth on the money list after the 1972 season, was regarded by many as a future star on the PGA Tour. He devoted himself to practice—he called it "polishing the rock"—and won a total of five times on the PGA Tour. The single most important event in his golfing career came at the Western Open in 1975. Heard was forced off the course when a storm halted play. He and playing partners Bobby Nichols and Lee Trevino opened their umbrellas and sat down beside a pond. They hadn't been there a minute when a bolt of lightning hit them. "I felt my hands clench so hard I couldn't open them," recalled Heard, twenty-five years later. "I actually thought to myself, 'I'll never play golf again.' "

While all three men were injured, Heard got the worst of it. Fluid had been burned out of the disks in his spinal cord, leaving him in so much pain whenever he moved that he spent two years in a hospital bed set up in the living room of his home. Though he tried to come back, and actually won the Atlanta Classic in 1978, he soon withdrew from regular competition. He took up work as a pro at a resort in Florida and, in 2001, became co-owner of a golf course north of Tampa.

Jim Jamieson's 1972 Western Open victory would be his only PGA Tour win. However, for three straight years he finished in the top sixty, and kept his playing privileges. In 1975 his hand was broken when he fell down a flight of stairs. The bones never healed properly, and Jamieson's swing never recovered. In the late 1970s he began a series of club jobs that included a stint at the prestigious Greenbriar resort. By 2001 he had become head instructor for the John Jacobs Golf Schools.

Gene Littler came back to the PGA Tour in 1973 and won that year's tournament in St. Louis. He would receive the Bob Jones award and the Hogan award in honor of his comeback. Littler won four more times, bringing his total victories on the regular tour to twenty-five. He joined the Senior PGA Tour and added another eight wins to his résumé. In 2001, at age seventy-one, he continued to play senior events and was sharp enough to score a 67 in tournament play.

Jack Nicklaus dominated professional golf through the decade of the seventies. He would win twenty-seven more times on the PGA Tour, bringing his total to seventy. He would capture five more professional Majors for a total of eighteen, the most in history. (If his two U.S. Amateur titles are included, the total is twenty.)

Nicklaus reached his goal of being recognized as a historic figure in sport and, at least so far, as the golfer with the greatest record of achievement ever. His last truly golden moment came with a win at the 1986 Masters, when he was forty-six years old.

In the 1990s Nicklaus played the Senior Tour and won ten times. However, he played a limited schedule and focused more on building a large complex of businesses with course design as the centerpiece. His design firm has opened more than two hundred courses, including a dozen that are widely considered to be among the top one hundred in the world.

As the millennium turned, Nicklaus was recognized not only as a golfer but as a super achiever among all athletes when *Sports Illustrated* named him the Individual Athlete of the Century. The competition included the likes of Muhammad Ali, Jesse Owens, and Joe Louis. His "golfer of the century"

awards came from the BBC, *GOLF Magazine,* the A[
Press, *Golfworld,* and *Golfweek.*

In a 2001 interview, Jack Nicklaus counted as per[
greatest accomplishment the fact that he had made a li[
of the game. "I enjoyed playing a game I loved, and I w[
to be the best I could possibly be at that game."

Near the end of 1972, **Arnold Palmer** stood in a loc[
room at Pinehurst, North Carolina, wearing nothing but h[
socks and underwear and vowed that he would take a hiatus
from golf until his putting returned. His putting never came
back, and as everyone who heard the vow expected, Palmer
never left golf. He loved the game, and the competition, too
much.

As the eldest of the greats of '72, Palmer slowed more
immediately than the others. He won the Bob Hope Desert
Classic in February 1973, but this lone victory did not signal
a revival of his greatness. In fact, he would never again win
on the regular PGA Tour. He would, however, take a dozen
titles on the Senior Tour, and several more in tournament
abroad. Though his winning days ended in the 1990s, Palmer
continued to play professionally, drawing the biggest crowds
of any senior player.

Palmer's business interests continued to grow. He purchased the golf course where his father was superintendent
and pro and, with some partners, acquired the Pebble Beach
Golf Links. His competition with Nicklaus continues in course
design. His firm has done roughly the same number of projects as the Nicklaus team, and is also a truly global endeavor.
His success in design and other businesses meant that in his
seventies he is still one of the wealthiest athletes in the world.

However, unlike his peers, Palmer remained attached to the small town where his life began. Every year he returns to Latrobe and conducts his business from a house-turned-headquarters across the street from the Latrobe Country Club.

Though age has not slowed Palmer much, illness has taken its toll. He underwent surgery for prostate cancer in 1997 and in the years that followed played fewer and fewer events. In November 1999 his wife, Winnie, with whom he eloped in 1957, died after a difficult battle with cancer. She was sixty-five years old. Palmer, who saw her through more than a year of serious illness, said, "She's the love of my life."

Gary Player, like his friend Palmer, has never stopped playing in tournaments and continues to use his past-winner status to enter certain prestige events such as the Masters. Though his nine Majors represent half the Nicklaus total, his one hundred worldwide tournament victories far exceeds the Nicklaus record.

Like many of his former competitors, Player operates a course design firm. He also owns golf equipment and accessory companies, and golf instruction facilities. But Player has not enjoyed the kind of business success enjoyed by the other two members of the Big Three.

As an international sports ambassador for South Africa, a philanthropist, and an advocate of racial equality, Player has exceeded all the golfers of his time in the realm of politics and human affairs. In July 2000, when *Golf Digest* picked the greatest golfers of the twentieth century, Gary Player was number eight. His tribute was written by Nelson Mandela.

After praising Player's efforts to integrate sport in South

Africa at substantial risk to himself, Mandela wrote, complishments as a humanitarian and statesman are e and may even surpass his accomplishments as an athlete. is a legacy that will last forever."

Doug Sanders won twenty times on the regular Tour but never captured a Major title. He would play on the Senior Tour for a decade but achieve only one victory, at the 1983 World Series Invitational. For seven years he was the host of one of the senior circuit's most successful events, the Doug Sanders Kingwood Senior Celebrity Classic.

In semiretirement, Sanders leads golf tours to Europe, is active promoting youth golf, and is building one of the largest collections of golf memorabilia in the world. More than three decades after he missed that short putt to lose the 1971 British Open, he confessed, "I'm not really over it, yet."

Lee Trevino did reach the million-dollar mark in tournament earnings, but he did not retire at age forty, fifty, or even sixty. He was, however, slowed significantly by the lightning strike that hit him and Jerry Heard in 1975. Like Heard, Trevino suffered back problems, but turned to surgery for help. His practice and playing time were limited, and his tournament play was affected. He wound up winning twenty-seven times on the regular tour. He netted five Majors, with the last coming in 1984 at the PGA Championship when he was forty-four years old.

In the 1980s Trevino endured substantial off-the-course turmoil. After years of disagreements that sometimes came to blows, he and his wife, Claudia, divorced. He suffered serious setbacks in business, due to conflicts with partners. And he chose to be a television commentator instead of a contestant at tour events. The formula nearly bankrupted him before he returned to competition on the Senior PGA Tour.

The Senior Tour was Trevino's salvation. In the 1990s he roared through the circuit, posting the most wins ever–twenty-eight–and taking player-of-the-year honors three times. He amassed his first million in prize money in his first year as a senior, 1990, and since then has exceeded $8 million. The value of his endorsements, for everything from golf equipment to Cadillac cars, soared along with his winnings.

As successful as Trevino was as a senior golfer, he was even more successful in his personal life once he hit middle age. He reduced and then simply stopped drinking entirely. In 1984 he was married for a third time, to a woman whose name is also Claudia, and found peace in a new family that includes a daughter born in 1989 and a son born in 1992. Mellowed and content, he came to credit Claudia II with much of his late success.

"Looking back, I think I might have been better than I thought I was at the time," noted Trevino during an interview. "As much as I talked, I had doubts, too. Now I can see that when I was on, I was as good as anyone out there."

Tom Weiskopf followed his success in 1972 with the best season of his career in 1973. In that season Weiskopf won five tournaments–including the British Open–in just eight weeks. Years later he would say that this run was inspired by the death of his father, which happened early in 1973.

"People wouldn't know this, but I do guilt real well," said Weiskopf in 2001. "I went out and tried to prove that I was the guy my father thought I should be. But I hated the notoriety, the superstar status. I never was comfortable with it."

A single Major victory was less than most of hi_
expected from Weiskopf. However, he once finished r
up in the U.S. Open and was third two times. He was
second at the Masters on four different occasions. He
fifteen victories on the regular PGA Tour. His last was at
prestigious Western Open, in 1982. A year later he reti_ed
from the regular tour at the relatively young age of forty-one.

"I may have had a few excellent years left, but I could feel
my skills were diminishing and my motivation was going."

After some years off, Weiskopf joined the Senior Tour.
He claimed four titles and close to $2 million before ending
his full-time commitment to tournament play in the late 1990s.
The year 2001 found Weiskopf out of competitive golf but
heavily involved in course design.

In the years that followed Tour '72, golf waited for a star to
equal Jack Nicklaus and a group of contenders who would re-
create the excitement of that year. At one time or another,
many young players appeared to be true successors to the likes
of Nicklaus, Palmer, Player, and Trevino.

Johnny Miller, who turned pro in 1969, possessed the kind
of swing, and power, that suggested true greatness. In 1973
he won his first Major, the U.S. Open, and in 1974 he won
eight tournaments in all. But by 1978, Miller had dropped
below one hundred on the tour money list, and his days of
dominance were over. He never approached the records held
by the great players of 1972.

After Miller came Tom Watson, who set a record by top-
ping the money list four years running, from 1977 to 1980.

Watson would win thirty-four regular tour titles and a remarkable five British Opens. Those Major victories included two direct confrontations with Nicklaus, and many believed he was the Golden Bear's true successor. Watson was truly exceptional, but in both regular wins and Major victories, he didn't approach the Nicklaus record, and he retired from the PGA Tour with only half as many titles.

Along with Watson, Seve Ballesteros, Greg Norman, Nick Faldo, and many others showed promise but fell short. In this same period, the professional game changed dramatically. The old barnstorming character of the tour disappeared completely, replaced by corporate wealth and stability. The education level of the typical pro changed, too, with nearly all pros going to college and half earning degrees. (In contrast, Nicklaus and Palmer had quit school before getting degrees. Trevino and Player never even enrolled.)

On the course, the power golf pioneered by Palmer and Nicklaus became the norm. By 1980, physical conditioning and the development of new equipment meant that pros routinely hit the ball 275 to 300 yards, and designers began lengthening courses to protect par. Players with the skills of a Buddy Allin, who were accurate but not powerful, could no longer compete.

Galleries were impressed by the skill and power of the pros of the 1990s. However, no single player came along to inspire them, as the greats of the early 1970s did, until Tiger Woods. Born in 1975, Eldrick "Tiger" Woods was groomed for golf greatness from the time he could hold a cut-down club. He posted Nicklaus's lifetime record on his wall and set about surpassing him. He succeeded as an amateur, and as pro received his idol's approval. After playing with Woods at Augusta National, Nicklaus offered the same words Bobby Jones used to describe Nicklaus as a youth. "He's playing a game with which I am not familiar."

As a pro, Woods has piled one victory onto another, including ten championships in 1999 alone. In the year 2000 he became the youngest player to have won all four Majors. As the 2001 tour season neared its end, Woods had compiled a career record of twenty-nine tour wins, including six Majors. He was not quite twenty-six years old, and with many more prime years left, he seemed on track to exceed Nicklaus's record in every category.

Although little doubt exists about Tiger's superior skills, it is also clear that today's pro tour does not offer the overall competitive drama seen in 1972. One by one players such as David Duval, Phil Mickelson, and Sergio Garcia have been nominated to challenge Tiger, but they have failed to develop into true rivals. The result is a pro game with one world-renowned superstar—Woods—but less to offer the fan who wants to see the sharpest competition. Nicklaus himself summed up the situation in early 2001.

"The guys I played against when I won most of my tournaments, guys like Palmer, Gary Player, Lee Trevino, and [later] Tom Watson were guys who had a history of winning Major championships." Nicklaus added, "Those guys were ready when you didn't win, and that doesn't seem to be the case now."

In 1972, Nicklaus's rivals defined his greatness most clearly. The world is still waiting for those competitors who will honor Tiger Woods in the same way.

AUTHOR'S NOTE

Dozens of professional golfers generously participated in what amounted to hundreds of hours of interviews for this book. Many also opened their scrapbooks and dug up records to confirm their memories. I was also aided by staff assistants to those players whose careers have become large enterprises. Along with Jack Nicklaus, Arnold Palmer, Gary Player, and Lee Trevino, those who helped in these ways included:

Brian Allin, Frank Beard, Al Besselink, Chuck Courtney, Bruce Crampton, Bruce Devlin, Lee Elder, Doug Ford, Marty Furgol, Bob Goalby, Paul Harney, Jerry Heard, Lionel Hebert, Jim Jamieson, Don January, Ted Kroll, Gene Littler, Charles Owens, Doug Sanders, and Tom Weiskopf.

Donald "Doc" Giffin, Putnam Pierman, Desmond Muirhead, Kaye Kessler, and Larry O'Brien, who were all eyewitnesses to golf history, acted as guides for my exploration. Help with the Masters was provided by Glenn J. Greenspan. Rand Jerris, historian of the United States Golf Association, shared the collection at Golf House and his keen observations.

David Barrett, of *GOLF Magazine,* went far beyond the call of friendship to provide unerring golf guidance. My editors, Gretchen Young and Will Schwalbe, gave me their unfailing support. Production editor David Lott lent me his patience and endurance. And my wife, Toni, was both counselor and compass. I am indebted to each of them.

INDEX